LOW CHOLESTEROL

Cookbook for Beginners

1600 Days of Nutritious & Delicious Recipes to Lower Cholesterol ,Protect Heart Healthy and Eating Well Every Day. Stress-Free 28-Day Meal Plan

April L. Wescott

CONTENTS

Fish And Seafood 37

Poultry 46

Pork And Beef Mains 56

Vegetarian Mains 65

Desserts And Treats 75

Appendix A : Measurement Conversions 84

Appendix B : Recipes Index 86

INTRODUCTION

In the expansive field of culinary arts, few radiate as radiantly as April L. Wescott. With an impressive career spanning over two decades, Wescott has always been at the forefront of redefining the boundaries of gastronomy. Her journey, marked by innovative recipes, culinary awards and memorable culinary experiences, took a turn when she faced personal health challenges related to elevated cholesterol levels. The experience led her to an illuminating exploration of heart-healthy eating without compromising flavor or style.

In The Low-Cholesterol Diet Cookbook, Westcott elegantly combines her culinary genius with a newfound passion for health and well-being. This isn't just another diet book; it's a weight loss book. It's a testament to Westcott's personal journey and a reflection of her commitment to ensuring that health concerns never get in the way of great food.

Westcott himself brings a deeply personal and informed perspective to this cookbook after grappling with the effects of high cholesterol. She recognizes the importance of diet in the management and prevention of heart-related diseases. However, she is also acutely aware of the joy and comfort that food brings to our lives, so dietary changes must not result in compromises in taste or the enjoyment of dining.

In this cookbook, readers embark on a heart-healthy culinary adventure. Each page is infused with Westcott's signature style, but with a renewed focus on ingredients and preparation techniques to meet the needs of those looking to lower their cholesterol. Packed with nutrition, flavor, and creativity, the recipes presented in this book will please foodies and the health-conscious alike.

From appetizers to main courses, from breakfast savory to midnight cravings, The Low Cholesterol Diet Cookbook offers a comprehensive guide for those who want to embark on a health-conscious culinary journey without giving up their love of fine food. Whether you're someone diagnosed with high cholesterol, someone looking to prevent future health problems, or just a passionate foodie looking for healthier options, this book will undoubtedly become your trusty kitchen companion.

As you turn each page, let April L. Wescott's expertise guide you, inspire you, and transform your kitchen into a sanctuary of health and culinary excellence. Welcome to the journey where every meal is an enjoyable, heart-healthy experience.

What is Cholesterol?

Cholesterol is a waxy, fat-like substance found in all cells of the body, essential for producing vitamin D, creating hormones, building cell membranes, and producing bile acids that help digest fat. While the body naturally produces all the cholesterol it needs, it's also obtained from dietary sources. Too much cholesterol in the blood, especially of the LDL (low-density lipoprotein) type, can lead to the buildup of plaques in arteries, increasing the risk of heart disease and stroke. In contrast, HDL (high-density lipoprotein) cholesterol helps protect against these conditions by transporting excess cholesterol back to the liver for excretion.

What affects Cholesterol levels?

1. **Diet**

Consuming saturated fats (found in red meat and full-fat dairy products) and trans fats (present in many processed foods) can raise LDL cholesterol. Dietary cholesterol, found in animal-based products, has a more minor effect on blood cholesterol for most people.

2. **Weight**

Being overweight can elevate bad LDL cholesterol and lower good HDL cholesterol levels. Losing weight can help correct these imbalances.

3. **Physical Activity**

Regular physical activity can raise HDL cholesterol and lower LDL cholesterol. At least 30 minutes of exercise a day can significantly impact cholesterol levels.

4. **Genetics**

Genes can influence how the body metabolizes LDL (bad) cholesterol. Familial hypercholesterolemia is a genetic disorder characterized by very high levels of cholesterol in the blood.

5. **Health Conditions**

Diseases such as diabetes or hypothyroidism can result in higher cholesterol levels.

6. **Medications**

Some drugs, like certain progestins, anabolic steroids, and corticosteroids, can increase bad LDL cholesterol and decrease good HDL cholesterol.

7. **Smoking**

Cigarette smoking damages blood vessels and lowers HDL cholesterol. The harmful effects of tobacco combined with high cholesterol heighten the risk of coronary artery disease.

8. **Alcohol**

In moderation, alcohol has been linked to higher levels of HDL cholesterol, but excessive consumption can lead to severe health problems, including high blood pressure, heart failure, and even strokes.

9. **Stress**

Prolonged stress can indirectly influence cholesterol levels by affecting lifestyle choices, such as diet and physical activity.

Risk of High Cholesterol

Coronary Heart Disease (CHD)

When there's too much LDL cholesterol in the bloodstream, it can build up on the walls of arteries, forming plaques. Over time, these plaques can narrow the arteries, leading to a condition called atherosclerosis. A narrowed coronary artery can hinder blood flow to the heart muscle, leading to CHD.

Heart Attack

If a plaque in a heart artery breaks, a blood clot forms around the plaque. This clot can block the flow of blood to the heart muscle, causing a heart attack.

Hypertension (High Blood Pressure)

The hardening and narrowing of the arteries due to plaque buildup can elevate blood pressure levels, which can further stress the heart and blood vessels.

Increased Risk of Diabetes

There's a bidirectional link between high cholesterol and diabetes. While diabetes can increase cholesterol levels, some research suggests that high cholesterol might also raise the risk of developing diabetes.

What are the benefits of a Low Cholesterol Diet?

- **Reduced Risk of Heart Diseases**

A diet low in cholesterol can reduce the buildup of plaques in arteries, thus minimizing the risk of atherosclerosis. This, in turn, reduces the chances of coronary artery disease and heart attacks.

- **Lowered Blood Pressure**

By preventing arterial plaque accumulation, a low cholesterol diet helps maintain smooth, flexible arteries which can contribute to controlled blood pressure.

- **Decreased Risk of Stroke**

Reducing cholesterol intake can prevent narrowing of arteries in the brain, which minimizes the risk of ischemic strokes.

- **Improved Blood Circulation**

Healthy arteries ensure better blood flow to all parts of the body, promoting optimal function of organs and tissues.

- **Weight Management**

Often, a diet that is low in cholesterol is also low in saturated fats and trans fats, which can help in weight reduction and maintenance.

- **Reduced Risk of Type 2 Diabetes**

Weight management and a diet low in saturated fats can reduce the risk of developing type 2 diabetes.

- **Healthy Liver Function**

The liver produces cholesterol, and a balanced diet can support its healthy function, preventing overproduction of cholesterol.

- **Overall Enhanced Well-being**

A balanced diet rich in fruits, vegetables, whole grains, and lean proteins—components of a low cholesterol diet—promotes overall health, energy, and vitality.

28 Day Meal Plan

	BREAKFAST	LUNCH	DINNER
Day 1	Nut Butter Overnight Oats 13	Creamy Tuna Sandwich 38	Wild Rice & Lentils 66
Day 2	Cinnamon Oat Bran Banana Pancakes 13	Salmon With Spicy Mixed Beans 38	Farro Sloppy Joes 66
Day 3	Cheddar-herb Biscuits 13	Poached Chilean Sea Bass With Pears 38	Cheese-and-veggie Stuffed Artichokes 67
Day 4	Cornmeal-cranberry Rolls 14	Grilled Scallops With Gremolata 39	Corn-and-chili Pancakes 67
Day 5	Applesauce Cinnamon Bread 14	Simple Pork Burgers 63	Spinach-ricotta Omelet 67
Day 6	Ciabatta Rolls 15	Sesame-pepper Salmon Kabobs 39	Tofu And Root Vegetable Curry 68
Day 7	"egg" Salad Sandwich Spread 15	Vietnamese Fish And Noodle Bowl 39	Pinto Bean Tortillas 68
Day 8	Apple-cinnamon Quinoa 15	Seared Scallops With Fruit 40	Crisp Polenta With Tomato Sauce 68
Day 9	Maghrebi Poached Eggs 15	Scallops On Skewers With Lemon 40	Ratatouille 69
Day 10	Savory Breakfast Rice Porridge 16	Roasted Shrimp And Veggies 40	Curried Garbanzo Beans 69
Day 11	Cranberry Orange Mixed Grain Granola 16	Baked Halibut In Mustard Sauce 41	Chickpeas In Lettuce Wraps 69
Day 12	Blueberry-walnut Muffins 16	Cajun-rubbed Fish 41	Baba Ghanoush With Fennel Stew 70
Day 13	Mango Tofu Smoothie 17	Poached Fish With Tomatoes And Capers 41	Chili-sautéed Tofu With Almonds 70
Day 14	Zucchini-walnut Bread 17	Tuna Patties 42	Sesame Soba Noodles 70

	BREAKFAST	LUNCH	DINNER
Day 15	Tuna-carrot Rice Balls 17	Crispy Mixed Nut Fish Fillets 42	Pumpkin And Chickpea Patties 71
Day 16	Spinach, Mushroom, And Egg White Omelet 18	Halibut Parcels 42	Kidney Bean Stew 71
Day 17	Salmon Soufflé 18	Catalán Salmon Tacos 43	Homestyle Bean Soup 72
Day 18	Cranberry-orange Bread 19	Flounder Fillet Bake 43	Savory French Toast 72
Day 19	Banana-blueberry Oatmeal Bread 19	Red Snapper Scampi 43	Quinoa-stuffed Peppers 72
Day 20	Ginger Pomegranate Sweet Tea 20	Sesame-crusted Mahi Mahi 44	Potato Soufflé 73
Day 21	Whole-grain Cornbread 20	Broiled Swordfish 44	Cannellini Bean–stuffed Sweet Potatoes 73
Day 22	Pumpkin Oatmeal Smoothies 20	Halibut Burgers 44	Spaghetti Squash Skillet 74
Day 23	Spicy Salsa Bruschetta 22	Shrimp Stir-fry 45	Sour-cream-and-herb Omelet 74
Day 24	Savory Chicken And Watermelon Rind Soup 22	Northwest Salmon 45	Balsamic Strawberry Yogurt 77
Day 25	Three Bean Soup 23	Iron Packed Turkey 47	Mustard Berry Vinaigrette 33
Day 26	Red-bean Salad With Taco Chips 23	Lime Turkey Skewers 47	Chimichurri Rub 33
Day 27	Broccoli Pasta Salad 24	Moroccan Chicken 47	Smoky Barbecue Rub 34
Day 28	Crunchy Cabbage And Carrot Salad 25	Italian Chicken Bake 48	Fresh Lime Salsa 36

| **Low Cholesterol** Cookbook

BREAKFAST AND BRUNCH

Nut Butter Overnight Oats

Servings: 1
Cooking Time: 3 Hours

Ingredients:

- ¾ cup low-fat milk
- ½ cup steel-cut oats
- 2 tablespoons nut butter (such as almond, cashew, or all-natural peanut butter)
- 1 tablespoon chia seeds
- 1 teaspoon maple syrup

Directions:

1. In a resealable container, mix the milk, oats, nut butter, chia seeds, and maple syrup.
2. Seal the container and place it in the refrigerator for three hours or overnight. Enjoy warm or cold.

Nutrition Info:

- Info Per Serving: Calories: 680 ; Fat: 28g ;Saturated fat: 5g ;Sodium: 86 mg

Cinnamon Oat Bran Banana Pancakes

Servings: 4
Cooking Time: 15 Minutes

Ingredients:

- 1 cup gluten-free flour blend (regular/ whole-wheat flour if you prefer)
- ⅓ cup oat bran
- 1 tablespoon brown sugar
- 1 teaspoon ground cinnamon
- ½ teaspoon baking powder
- ½ teaspoon baking soda
- 1 small banana, peeled and mashed
- ⅔ cup low-fat milk
- 1 egg, separated
- 1 tablespoon canola oil

Directions:

1. In a medium bowl, combine the flour, oat bran, brown sugar, cinnamon, baking powder, and baking soda and mix well with a wire whisk.
2. In another medium bowl, combine the banana, milk, and egg yolk, and beat until well combined.
3. In another medium bowl, beat the egg white with an electric mixer until stiff peaks form.
4. Add the banana mixture to the flour mixture and stir just until combined. Do not overmix.
5. Fold in the beaten egg white.
6. Heat a nonstick griddle or large skillet over medium heat, add the oil, and swirl it around the pan. When the pan is hot enough that a drop of water skitters on the surface, pour a scant ¼ cup of the batter onto the griddle. Repeat to just fill the pan.
7. Cook the pancakes until the edges start to look lightly browned and bubbles form on the surface, about 2 minutes. Flip the pancakes and cook for 1 to 2 minutes longer or until the bottoms are browned. Serve immediately.

Nutrition Info:

- Info Per Serving: Calories: 245 ; Fat: 6 g ;Saturated fat: 3 g ;Sodium: 241 mg

Cheddar-herb Biscuits

Servings: 8
Cooking Time: X

Ingredients:

- 1½ cups all-purpose flour
- ½ cup whole wheat flour
- 1½ teaspoons baking powder
- ½ teaspoon baking soda
- ¼ teaspoon garlic salt
- ¼ cup canola oil
- 1 egg white
- 2/3 cup buttermilk
- 1 cup grated low-fat extra-sharp Cheddar cheese
- 1 tablespoon chopped fresh rosemary
- 1 tablespoons fresh thyme leaves
- 1 tablespoon butter or plant sterol margarine, melted
- 1 tablespoon chopped flat-leaf parsley

Directions:

1. Preheat oven to 400ºF. Line a cookie sheet with parchment paper and set aside.
2. In large bowl, combine flour, whole-wheat flour, baking powder, baking soda, and garlic salt and mix well. In small bowl, combine oil, egg white, and buttermilk. Add all at once to dry ingredients, stirring just until moistened.

3. Fold in cheese, rosemary, and thyme leaves. Drop into eight mounds onto prepared cookie sheet. Bake for 15–20 minutes or until biscuits are light golden brown.

4. In small microwave-safe bowl, melt butter. Add parsley and stir well. Brush this mixture over the hot biscuits. Remove biscuits to wire rack to cool slightly before serving.

Nutrition Info:

• Info Per Serving: Calories: 218.86; Fat:9.80 g ;Saturated fat:2.18 g ;Sodium: 272.53 mg

Cornmeal-cranberry Rolls

Servings: 18
Cooking Time: X

Ingredients:

• ½ cup buttermilk
• ½ cup water
• ½ cup yellow cornmeal
• 1/3 cup canola oil
• 2½ to 3½ cups all-purpose flour
• 1 (¼-ounce) package instant-blend dried yeast
• ½ teaspoon salt
• 1 egg
• 2 egg whites
• 1/3 cup honey
• 2/3 cup chopped dried cranberries
• 2 tablespoons butter, melted

Directions:

1. In medium saucepan, combine buttermilk, water, cornmeal, and oil over medium heat. Cook, stirring, until very warm. Remove from heat.

2. In large bowl, combine 2 cups flour, yeast, and salt and mix well. Add the buttermilk mixture along with egg, egg whites, and honey. Beat for 2 minutes. Then gradually add enough remaining flour until a stiff batter forms. Stir in cranberries.

3. Cover and let rise until doubled, about 1 hour. Grease 18 muffin cups with nonstick cooking spray. Spoon batter into the prepared cups, filling each full. Cover and let rise for 30 minutes.

4. Preheat oven to 350ºF. Bake rolls for 20–30 minutes or until golden brown and set. Immediately brush with butter. Remove from pans and let cool on wire racks.

Nutrition Info:

• Info Per Serving: Calories: 194.31; Fat:6.20 g ;Saturated fat: 1.37g ;Sodium:113.41 mg

Applesauce Cinnamon Bread

Servings: 12
Cooking Time: X

Ingredients:

• 1¼ cups applesauce
• 1 cup brown sugar, divided
• 1/3 cup canola oil
• ¼ cup skim milk
• ½ cup liquid egg substitute
• 1 cup all-purpose flour
• ¼ cup whole-wheat flour
• 2 tablespoons wheat germ
• 1½ teaspoons cinnamon, divided
• ½ teaspoon nutmeg
• 1 teaspoon baking powder
• ½ teaspoon baking soda
• ½ cup golden raisins
• ½ cup chopped walnuts

Directions:

1. Preheat oven to 350ºF. Spray a 9" × 5" loaf pan with nonstick cooking spray containing flour, and set aside.

2. In large bowl, combine applesauce, ¼ cup plus 2 tablespoons brown sugar, canola oil, milk, and egg substitute and beat well.

3. In medium bowl, combine flour, whole-wheat flour, wheat germ, 1 teaspoon cinnamon, nutmeg, baking powder, baking soda, raisins, and walnuts, and mix well. Add to applesauce mixture and stir until combined.

4. Pour batter into prepared pan. In small bowl, combine remaining 2 tablespoons brown sugar with remaining ½ teaspoon cinnamon and mix well. Sprinkle evenly over batter in pan. Bake for 55–65 minutes or until bread is golden-brown and toothpick inserted in center comes out clean. Remove from pan and let cool on wire

Nutrition Info:

• Info Per Serving: Calories: 263.33; Fat:9.88 g ;Saturated fat:0.75g ;Sodium:113.09 mg

Ciabatta Rolls

Servings: 6
Cooking Time: X

Ingredients:
- 1 recipe Whole-Grain Ciabatta
- 2 tablespoons olive oil
- 3 tablespoons cornmeal

Directions:
1. Prepare Ciabatta through the first rising. Punch down dough and turn onto lightly floured surface.
2. Divide dough into 6 portions. Using floured fingers, shape each portion into a 3" × 3" rectangle. Grease six 4" × 4" squares on a cookie sheet with olive oil and sprinkle with cornmeal. Place dough onto each cornmeal coated square. Drizzle with remaining olive oil.
3. Let rise in warm place until doubled in size, about 45 minutes. Preheat oven to 425ºF. Bake rolls for 10–15 minutes or until very light brown. Turn off oven and prop open oven door. Let rolls stand in oven for another 5 minutes. Then remove from oven and let cool on wire racks.

Nutrition Info:
- Info Per Serving: Calories:283.00 ; Fat: 6.17 g ;Saturated fat:0.91 g ;Sodium: 203.58 mg

"egg" Salad Sandwich Spread

Servings: 6
Cooking Time: X

Ingredients:
- ½ (12-ounce) package firm tofu
- 1/3 cup low-fat mayonnaise
- 2 tablespoons plain yogurt
- 2 tablespoons Dijon mustard
- 1/8 teaspoon pepper
- ½ teaspoon dried oregano leaves
- 1 cup chopped celery
- 1 red bell pepper, chopped
- ¼ cup grated Parmesan cheese

Directions:
1. Drain tofu and drain again on paper towels, pressing to remove moisture. Set aside.
2. In medium bowl, combine remaining ingredients and stir gently to combine. Crumble tofu into bowl and mix until mixture looks like egg salad. Cover tightly and refrigerate for 2–3 hours before serving. Store, covered, in the refrigerator for 3–4 days.

Nutrition Info:
- Info Per Serving: Calories: 105.78; Fat: 7.17g ;Saturated fat: 1.71 g ;Sodium: 235.50 mg

Apple-cinnamon Quinoa

Servings: 1
Cooking Time: 12 Minutes

Ingredients:
- 1¼ cups low-fat milk
- 1 cup diced apple, divided
- ½ cup quinoa
- 1 teaspoon ground cinnamon
- 1 teaspoon maple syrup

Directions:
1. In a medium saucepan over medium heat, place the milk, ½ cup of apple, the quinoa, and cinnamon and bring to a boil. Reduce the heat to low, partially cover, and simmer until all the liquid evaporates, about 12 minutes.
2. Transfer the quinoa mixture to a bowl and top with the remaining diced apple and maple syrup. Serve.

Nutrition Info:
- Info Per Serving: Calories: 521; Fat: 3g ;Saturated fat: 0g ;Sodium: 141mg

Maghrebi Poached Eggs

Servings: 4
Cooking Time: 25 Min

Ingredients:
- 1 tbsp. avocado oil
- 1 medium red bell pepper, chopped
- 1 (28 oz) can low-sodium diced tomatoes
- 1 tsp ground cumin
- Fine sea salt
- Ground black pepper
- 4 large free-range eggs
- ¼ cup cilantro, chopped

Directions:
1. Heat the avocado oil in a large heavy-bottom pan over medium-high heat.
2. Add the red bell pepper and cook for 4 to 6 minutes, until softened.
3. Add the tomatoes with the juice and cumin. Cook for 10 minutes, or until the flavor comes together and the sauce has thickened. Season with salt and pepper to taste.
4. Use a large spoon to make 4 depressions in the to-

mato mixture. Carefully crack an egg into each depression. Cover the pan and cook for 5 to 7 minutes, or until the eggs are cooked to your liking. Remove from the heat.

5. Divide into 4 bowls and garnish with chopped cilantro. Serve while hot.

Nutrition Info:
- Info Per Serving: Calories: 146 ; Fat: 9 g ;Saturated fat: 2 g ;Sodium: 102 mg

Savory Breakfast Rice Porridge

Servings: 5
Cooking Time: 1 Hour 5 Minutes

Ingredients:
- 1 pound firm tofu, drained and sliced into 1-inch cubes
- 2 tablespoons low-sodium soy sauce
- 1 tablespoon minced garlic
- 9 cups water
- 1 cup rinsed uncooked brown rice
- 1 cup chopped spinach
- Sea salt
- Freshly ground black pepper

Directions:
1. In a medium bowl, place the tofu, soy sauce, and garlic. Let marinate in the refrigerator for 30 minutes.
2. While the tofu is marinating, in a large saucepan, combine the water and brown rice and bring to a boil over high heat, then reduce the heat to medium-high and simmer for 60 minutes, whisking occasionally.
3. Whisk the cooked rice porridge to your desired consistency.
4. Add the tofu and the marinade to the porridge and bring it to a boil, then simmer for 2 to 3 minutes, until fragrant.
5. Stir in the spinach and season with salt and pepper. Serve warm.

Nutrition Info:
- Info Per Serving: Calories: 276 ; Fat: 9g ;Saturated fat: 1 g ;Sodium: 255mg

Cranberry Orange Mixed Grain Granola

Servings: 6
Cooking Time: 20 Minutes

Ingredients:
- 1 cup regular rolled oats
- ½ cup barley flakes

- 1 cup kamut flakes or corn or wheat flakes
- ⅓ cup sunflower seeds
- 3 tablespoons pure maple syrup
- 1 tablespoon safflower oil
- 1 tablespoon orange juice
- 1 teaspoon vanilla extract
- 2 teaspoons fresh orange zest
- ½ cup chopped dried cranberries

Directions:
1. Preheat the oven to 350°F.
2. In a large bowl, combine the rolled oats, barley flakes, kamut flakes, and sunflower seeds.
3. In a small bowl, combine the maple syrup, safflower oil, orange juice, vanilla, and orange zest, mixing well.
4. Drizzle the maple syrup mixture over the grains and toss to coat.
5. Spread the mixture in a baking sheet.
6. Bake for 15 to 20 minutes, stirring once, until the mixture is lightly toasted.
7. Stir in the cranberries, let the granola cool completely, and store in an airtight container at room temperature for up to 1 week.

Nutrition Info:
- Info Per Serving: Calories: 226 ; Fat: 8 g ;Saturated fat: 1 g ;Sodium: 47 mg

Blueberry-walnut Muffins

Servings: 12
Cooking Time: X

Ingredients:
- 1 cup buttermilk
- 1 egg
- 2 egg whites
- 6 tablespoons canola oil
- ½ cup sugar
- 1/8 teaspoon salt
- 1¼ cups all-purpose flour
- ¼ cup whole-wheat flour
- 1 teaspoon baking powder
- 1 teaspoon baking soda
- 1 cup blueberries
- 1 tablespoon flour
- ½ cup chopped walnuts
- 2 tablespoons brown sugar
- ½ teaspoon cinnamon

Directions:
1. Preheat oven to 400ºF. Line 12 muffin cups with

paper liners and set aside. In large bowl, combine buttermilk, egg, egg whites, oil, sugar, and salt and mix well.

2. Stir in 1¼ cups flour, whole-wheat flour, baking powder, and baking soda just until dry ingredients are moistened. In small bowl, toss blueberries with 1 tablespoon flour. Stir into batter along with walnuts.

3. Fill prepared muffin cups ¼ full. In small bowl, combine 2 tablespoons brown sugar and cinnamon and sprinkle over muffins. Bake for 17–22 minutes or until golden-brown and set. Remove from muffin cups and cool on wire racks.

Nutrition Info:
- Info Per Serving: Calories: 230.36; Fat:10.80 g ;Saturated fat:0.95 g ;Sodium: 197.52 mg

Mango Tofu Smoothie

Servings: 3
Cooking Time: 5 Minutes

Ingredients:
- 1 banana
- 1 cup mango, fresh or frozen
- ¾ cup soft tofu
- ½ cup orange juice
- ½ cup low-fat milk

Directions:
1. In a blender, place the banana, mango, soft tofu, orange juice, and milk and blend until smooth, about 30 seconds to 1 minute. Serve immediately.

Nutrition Info:
- Info Per Serving: Calories:143 ; Fat:3g ;Saturated fat: 1g;Sodium: 25mg

Zucchini-walnut Bread

Servings: 12
Cooking Time: X

Ingredients:
- ¼ cup canola oil
- ¼ cup sugar
- ½ cup brown sugar
- 1 egg
- 2 egg whites
- ½ cup orange juice
- 2 teaspoons vanilla
- 1 cup grated zucchini
- 1 teaspoon grated lemon zest
- 2 tablespoons wheat germ
- 1 cup all-purpose flour
- 1 cup whole-wheat flour
- 1 teaspoon baking powder
- ½ teaspoon baking soda
- 1/8 teaspoon salt
- 1 teaspoon cinnamon
- ¼ teaspoon cloves
- ½ cup chopped walnuts

Directions:
1. Preheat oven to 350ºF. Spray a 9" × 5" loaf pan with nonstick cooking spray containing flour, and set aside.

2. In large bowl, combine oil, sugar, brown sugar, egg, egg whites, orange juice, and vanilla and beat until smooth. Stir in zucchini, lemon zest, and wheat germ.

3. Sift together flour, whole-wheat flour, baking powder, baking soda, salt, cinnamon, and cloves, and add to oil mixture. Stir just until combined, then fold in walnuts. Pour into prepared pan.

4. Bake for 55–65 minutes or until bread is golden-brown and toothpick inserted in center comes out clean. Remove from pan and let cool on wire rack.

Nutrition Info:
- Info Per Serving: Calories:217.46 ; Fat: 8.48 g ;Saturated fat:0.70 g;Sodium: 127.63 mg

Tuna-carrot Rice Balls

Servings: 1
Cooking Time: 35 Minutes

Ingredients:
- ¼ cup short-grain brown rice, rinsed
- ¾ cup water, divided
- ½ cup diced carrots
- 1 (2½-ounce) can low-sodium tuna packed in water, drained
- ½ teaspoon sesame oil
- Sea salt
- Freshly ground black pepper
- 2 (4-by-5-inch) sheets dried seaweed

Directions:
1. Combine the rice and ½ cup water in a medium saucepan over high heat and bring to a boil. Cover, reduce the heat to low, and simmer until the liquid is absorbed, about 30 minutes. Remove from the heat, fluff with a fork, and let cool slightly.

2. Place the carrots and the remaining ¼ cup water in a medium skillet over medium heat and cook until the carrots soften, about 3 minutes. Remove the skillet

from the heat.

3. Add the tuna, sesame oil, salt, and pepper to the skillet and mix thoroughly.

4. Place the cooked rice in a medium bowl and stir in the tuna mixture.

5. Wet your hands with water and shape the mixture into 2 separate rice balls.

6. Wrap 1 sheet of seaweed around each rice ball and serve.

Nutrition Info:
- Info Per Serving: Calories:158 ; Fat: 2g ;Saturated fat: 0g ;Sodium: 224mg

Hot Pepper And Salsa Frittata

Servings: 3
Cooking Time: X

Ingredients:
- 2 tablespoons olive oil
- ½ cup finely chopped red onion
- 1 jalapeño pepper, minced
- ½ cup egg substitute
- 4 egg whites
- ¼ cup skim milk
- 3 tablespoons grated Parmesan cheese
- ½ cup Super Spicy Salsa (page 85)
- 2 tablespoons chopped cilantro

Directions:
1. In large nonstick skillet, heat olive oil over medium heat. Add onion and jalapeño pepper; cook and stir until crisp-tender, about 4 minutes.

2. Meanwhile, in medium bowl beat egg substitute, egg whites, milk, and cheese until combined. Pour into skillet. Cook, running spatula around edge of frittata as it cooks, until eggs are soft set and light brown on the bottom.

3. Preheat broiler. Place frittata 6" from heat and broil for 4–7 minutes, watching carefully, until the top is browned and set. Top with salsa and cilantro and serve immediately.

Nutrition Info:
- Info Per Serving: Calories: 201.08;Fat: 201.08 ;Saturated fat: 2.67 g;Sodium: 289.79 mg

Spinach, Mushroom, And Egg White Omelet

Servings: 2
Cooking Time: 5 Minutes

Ingredients:
- 2 cups chopped fresh spinach
- ½ cup diced white mushrooms
- 2 tablespoons water
- 1 tablespoon minced garlic
- Pinch salt
- 1 teaspoon olive oil, divided
- 1½ cups liquid egg whites, divided

Directions:
1. In a large skillet over medium heat, place the spinach, mushrooms, water, garlic, and salt, and cook for about 2 minutes until fragrant. Transfer the vegetable mixture to a medium bowl.

2. Heat half the olive oil in the skillet. Cook ¾ cup egg whites for about 3 minutes, or until firm.

3. Use a spoon to scoop half of the vegetable mixture onto one side of the omelet and fold it over. Transfer the omelet to a plate and repeat with the remaining olive oil, egg white, and vegetable mixture. Serve immediately.

Nutrition Info:
- Info Per Serving: Calories: 132 ; Fat: 3 g ;Saturated fat: 0 g ;Sodium: 405 mg

Salmon Soufflé

Servings: 4
Cooking Time: X

Ingredients:
- 1 (7-ounce) can salmon, drained
- 1 tablespoon olive oil
- ½ cup finely chopped red onion
- 2 tablespoons lemon juice
- ½ teaspoon dried dill weed
- 8 egg whites
- ¼ teaspoon cream of tartar
- ¼ cup low-fat mayonnaise
- 1/8 teaspoon cayenne pepper

Directions:
1. Preheat oven to 400ºF. Remove skin and bones from salmon; flake salmon and set aside.

2. In small pan, heat olive oil over medium heat. Add onion; cook and stir until tender, about 5 minutes. Re-

move from heat and add salmon, lemon juice, and dill weed; do not stir, but set aside.

3. In large bowl, combine egg whites with cream of tartar; beat until stiff peaks form. Add mayonnaise and pepper to salmon mixture and mix gently.

4. Fold egg whites into salmon mixture. Spray the bottom of a 2-quart casserole with nonstick cooking spray. Pour salmon mixture into dish. Bake for 20 minutes, then lower heat to 350ºF and bake for 20–30 minutes longer or until soufflé is puffed and deep golden brown. Serve immediately.

Nutrition Info:
- Info Per Serving: Calories:203.36 ;Fat: 11.28 gr ;Saturated fat: 1.96 g;Sodium: 255.03 mg

Cranberry-orange Bread

Servings: 12
Cooking Time: X

Ingredients:
- ¼ cup orange juice
- 2 tablespoons frozen orange juice concentrate, thawed
- ½ teaspoon almond extract
- ¼ cup canola oil
- 1 egg
- 1/3 cup sugar
- ½ cup brown sugar
- 1 teaspoon grated orange zest
- 1½ cups all-purpose flour
- ¼ cup whole-wheat flour
- 1 teaspoon baking soda
- 1 teaspoon baking powder
- 2 cups chopped cranberries
- ½ cup chopped hazelnuts

Directions:
1. Preheat oven to 350ºF. Spray a 9" × 5" loaf pan with nonstick cooking spray containing flour, and set aside.

2. In medium bowl, combine orange juice, orange juice concentrate, almond extract, canola oil, egg, sugar, brown sugar, and orange zest and beat to combine.

3. In large bowl, combine flour, whole-wheat flour, baking soda, baking powder, and mix. Make a well in the center of the flour mixture and pour in the orange juice mixture. Stir just until dry ingredients are moistened.

4. Fold in cranberries and hazelnuts. Pour into prepared pan. Bake for 55–65 minutes or until bread is golden-brown and toothpick inserted in center comes out clean. Remove from pan and let cool on wire rack.

Nutrition Info:
- Info Per Serving: Calories: 232.48; Fat: 8.24 g ;Saturated fat:0.72g ;Sodium: 145.81 mg

Banana-blueberry Oatmeal Bread

Servings: 12
Cooking Time: X

Ingredients:
- 1 (3-ounce) package light cream cheese, softened
- ¼ cup brown sugar
- ¼ cup sugar
- 2 bananas, mashed
- 1 egg
- 2 egg whites
- ¼ cup orange juice
- 1 cup all-purpose flour
- ½ cup whole-wheat flour
- 1 teaspoon baking powder
- 1 teaspoon baking soda
- 1 cup blueberries
- ½ cup regular oatmeal

Directions:
1. Preheat oven to 350ºF. Spray a 9" × 5" loaf pan with nonstick cooking spray containing flour, and set aside.

2. In large bowl, combine cream cheese with brown sugar and sugar and beat until fluffy. Beat in mashed bananas, then add egg, egg whites, and orange juice and beat until smooth.

3. Stir together flour, whole-wheat flour, baking powder, and baking soda. Add to batter and stir just until combined. Fold in blueberries and oatmeal. Pour into prepared loaf pan.

4. Bake for 50–60 minutes or until bread is deep golden-brown and toothpick inserted in center comes out clean. Remove from pan and cool on wire rack.

Nutrition Info:
- Info Per Serving: Calories: 165.78 ; Fat:2.43 g ;Saturated fat: 1.05 g ;Sodium: 173.82 mg

Ginger Pomegranate Sweet Tea

Servings: 4
Cooking Time: 4 Minutes

Ingredients:

- 2 cups unsweetened pomegranate juice
- 2 slices peeled ginger root, roughly chopped
- 2 cups water
- 2 bags herbal or green tea
- 1 tablespoon honey
- 1 tablespoon fresh lemon juice
- ½ teaspoon ground cinnamon

Directions:

1. Combine the pomegranate juice, ginger root, and water in a medium nonreactive saucepan.
2. Bring the mixture to a simmer over medium heat. Reduce the heat to low and simmer for 2 minutes.
3. Remove the pan from the heat and add the tea bags. Let steep for 2 minutes. Stir in the honey, lemon juice and cinnamon.
4. Strain the mixture into a teapot or glass serving container, discarding the tea bags and solids. Serve immediately.

Nutrition Info:

- Info Per Serving: Calories: 85 ; Fat: 0 g ;Saturated fat: 0 g ;Sodium: 12 mg

Whole-grain Cornbread

Servings: 9
Cooking Time: X

Ingredients:

- ¼ cup all-purpose flour
- ½ cup whole-wheat flour
- ¼ cup brown sugar
- 2 teaspoons baking powder
- 1 teaspoon baking soda
- 1 cup cornmeal
- 1/3 cup oat bran
- 1 egg
- 2 egg whites
- ¼ cup honey
- 1 cup buttermilk
- ¼ cup canola oil

Directions:

1. Preheat oven to 400ºF. Spray a 9" square pan with nonstick cooking spray containing flour, and set aside. In large mixing bowl, combine flour, whole-wheat flour, brown sugar, baking powder, baking soda, cornmeal, and oat bran and mix well.
2. In small bowl, combine egg, egg whites, honey, buttermilk, and canola oil and beat to combine. Add to dry ingredients and stir just until mixed.
3. Spoon into prepared pan and smooth top. Bake for 25–35 minutes or until bread is golden brown.

Nutrition Info:

- Info Per Serving: Calories: 252.79; Fat:7.58 g ;Saturated fat:0.87 g ;Sodium: 272.96 mg

Pumpkin Oatmeal Smoothies

Servings: X
Cooking Time: X

Ingredients:

- 2 cups unsweetened soy milk
- 1 cup puréed canned pumpkin
- ½ cup rolled oats
- 1 tablespoon hemp hearts
- 1 tablespoon blackstrap molasses
- ¼ teaspoon ground cinnamon
- ⅛ teaspoon ground nutmeg
- ⅛ teaspoon ground ginger

Directions:

1. In a blender, add the soy milk, pumpkin, oats, hemp hearts, molasses, cinnamon, nutmeg, and ginger and purée until smooth.
2. Pour into glasses and serve immediately.

Nutrition Info:

- Info Per Serving: Calories: 322; Fat: 9 g ;Saturated fat: 1 g ;Sodium: 136 mg

SOUPS, SALADS, AND SIDES

Soups, Salads, And Sides

Spicy Salsa Bruschetta

Servings: 12
Cooking Time: X

Ingredients:
- 12 (½-inch thick) slices Hearty-Grain French Bread
- 3 tablespoons olive oil
- ½ cup part-skim ricotta cheese
- 1 cup Super Spicy Salsa

Directions:
1. Preheat broiler. Brush bread slices on both sides with olive oil and place on broiler pan. Broil 6" from heat until golden brown, about 3–5 minutes, then turn and broil the second side until golden brown, about 3–5 minutes.
2. Spread each toasted bread slice with 2 teaspoons ricotta cheese, then top with a spoonful of salsa. Serve immediately.

Nutrition Info:
- Info Per Serving: Calories: 99.90; Fat: 4.86 g ;Saturated fat: 1.21 g ;Sodium: 57.35 mg

Savory Chicken And Watermelon Rind Soup

Servings: 4
Cooking Time: 35 Minutes

Ingredients:
- 1 tablespoon olive oil
- ¾ pound boneless, skinless chicken thighs
- 2 tablespoons minced garlic
- 1 teaspoon peeled minced fresh ginger
- Pinch sea salt
- Pinch freshly ground black pepper
- 6 cups water
- 3 cups diced watermelon rind

Directions:
1. In a large stockpot, heat the olive oil over medium heat. Add the chicken, garlic, ginger, salt, and pepper, and sauté until the chicken is no longer pink, about 5 minutes.
2. Add the water to the pot, increase the heat to high, and bring the soup to a boil.
3. Add the watermelon rind once the water comes to a boil.
4. Allow the soup to come to a boil again, reduce the heat to medium, and simmer for 30 minutes.
5. Add more salt, if desired, and enjoy immediately.

Nutrition Info:
- Info Per Serving: Calories: 157 ; Fat: 7 g ;Saturated fat: 1g ;Sodium: 121 mg

Citrus Sparagus

Servings: 2
Cooking Time: 5 Min

Ingredients:
- ½ tsp olive oil
- ½ cup walnuts, finely chopped
- ½ lime, juiced and zested
- Himalayan pink salt
- Ground black pepper
- ½ lb. asparagus, woody ends trimmed

Directions:
1. Warm the olive oil in a small-sized, nonstick frying pan, over medium heat.
2. Add the walnuts and fry for 4 minutes until fragrant and golden brown.
3. Remove the pan from the heat and mix in the lime zest and juice.
4. Season the walnut mixture with salt and pepper to taste, set aside.
5. Fill a medium-sized stockpot with water and bring to the boil over high heat.
6. Blanch the asparagus for 2 minutes until al dente.
7. Discard the water and arrange the asparagus on a serving plate.
8. Sprinkle the walnut topping over the vegetables and serve.

Nutrition Info:
- Info Per Serving: Calories: 192 ; Fat:15 g ;Saturated fat: 1 g ;Sodium: 10 mg

Five-onion Soup

Servings: 4
Cooking Time: X

Ingredients:
- 2 tablespoons olive oil
- 1 red onion, chopped
- 1 Vidalia or Walla Walla onion, chopped
- 2 shallots, chopped
- 4 scallions, chopped
- 4 cloves garlic, chopped
- 1 teaspoon sugar
- 4 cups Low-Sodium Beef Broth
- 2 bay leaves
- 1 tablespoon Worcestershire sauce
- 1 cup dry red wine
- ¼ teaspoon pepper
- 4 slices Hearty-Grain French Bread
- ½ cup shredded Muenster cheese

Directions:
1. In large soup pot, heat olive oil over medium heat. Add red onion, Vidalia onion, shallots, scallions, and garlic; cook and stir for 15–20 minutes or until onions are very soft. Sprinkle with sugar and continue cooking for 5–10 minutes longer until the onions start to caramelize and turn brown at the edges.
2. Add beef broth, bay leaves, Worcestershire sauce, wine, and pepper and bring to a simmer. Reduce heat to low, cover, and simmer for one hour.
3. When ready to serve, toast the French bread slices in a toaster oven or under the broiler. Divide cheese among bread slices and toast again just until the cheese melts. Pour soup into bowls and top with bread; serve immediately.

Nutrition Info:
- Info Per Serving: Calories: 357.41 ; Fat: 15.34 g ;Saturated fat: 5.72 g;Sodium: 254.39 mg

Three Bean Soup

Servings: 4
Cooking Time: 20 Minutes

Ingredients:
- 1 tablespoon olive oil
- 1 leek, white and light-green parts, chopped and rinsed
- 1 carrot, thinly sliced
- 1 (16-ounce) can low-sodium black beans, rinsed and drained
- 2 cups green beans, cut into 1-inch pieces
- 1 cup frozen shelled edamame
- 3 cups low-sodium vegetable broth
- 1 (14-ounce) can no-salt-added diced tomatoes
- 1 teaspoon dried basil leaves
- 1 teaspoon dried oregano leaves
- Pinch salt
- ⅛ teaspoon black pepper

Directions:
1. In a large saucepan or stockpot, heat the olive oil over medium heat.
2. Add the leek, and cook and stir for 4 minutes. Add the carrot, and cook and stir for 1 minute.
3. Add the black beans, green beans, edamame, vegetable broth, tomatoes, basil, oregano, salt, and pepper, stir to combine, and bring to a boil.
4. Reduce the heat to low, partially cover the pan, and simmer for 15 minutes or until the vegetables are tender. Serve.

Nutrition Info:
- Info Per Serving: Calories:245; Fat: 6g ;Saturated fat: 1g ;Sodium:260 mg

Red-bean Salad With Taco Chips

Servings: 6
Cooking Time: X

Ingredients:
- ¼ cup lime juice
- ½ cup low-fat sour cream
- ½ cup plain yogurt
- ½ teaspoon crushed red pepper flakes
- 1 red onion, chopped
- 2 jalapeño peppers, minced
- 1 green bell pepper, chopped
- 3 stalks celery, chopped
- 4 cups Beans for Soup
- 6 cups shredded lettuce
- ½ cup pumpkin seeds
- 2 cups crushed low-fat taco chips

Directions:
1. In large bowl combine lime juice, sour cream, yogurt, pepper flakes, onion, and jalapeño peppers; mix well. Add bell pepper, celery, and beans and mix well. This can be chilled, well covered, until ready to eat.
2. When ready to serve, arrange lettuce on a serving platter and spoon the bean mixture over all. Sprinkle with pumpkin seeds and crushed taco chips and serve immediately.

Nutrition Info:
- Info Per Serving: Calories:324.28 ; Fat:8.60 g ;Saturated fat:2.83 g ;Sodium: 204.12 mg

Broccoli Pasta Salad

Servings: 8–10
Cooking Time: X

Ingredients:
- 1/3 cup balsamic vinegar
- 3 tablespoons olive oil
- 1 tablespoon walnut oil
- ½ cup low-fat mayonnaise
- 2 tablespoons Dijon mustard
- 2 tablespoons lemon juice
- 2 cloves garlic, minced
- 4 shallots, minced
- 1/8 teaspoon pepper
- 1 (16-ounce) package farfalle pasta
- 1 head broccoli
- ½ cup walnut pieces, toasted
- 1/3 cup grated Parmesan cheese

Directions:
1. Bring a large pot of water to a boil. Meanwhile, in large bowl combine vinegar, olive oil, walnut oil, mayonnaise, mustard, lemon juice, garlic, shallots, and pepper, and mix well.
2. Add pasta to water and stir. Meanwhile, rinse broccoli and cut off florets. When pasta has cooked for 6 minutes, add the broccoli and stir. Bring back to a boil and cook for 3–5 minutes or until pasta is tender and broccoli is crisp-tender. Drain well and add immediately to vinegar mixture.
3. Toss to coat; let stand for 10 minutes so pasta will absorb some of the dressing. Sprinkle with walnuts and Parmesan and serve.

Nutrition Info:
- Info Per Serving: Calories:346.85; Fat:15.11g ;Saturated fat: 2.23 g ;Sodium: 195.68 mg

Snow Peas With Shallots

Servings: 4
Cooking Time: X

Ingredients:
- 1 pound snow peas
- 2 tablespoons olive oil
- 4 shallots, minced
- ½ pound cremini mushrooms, sliced
- 2 tablespoons sherry vinegar
- 1 teaspoon lemon juice

Directions:
1. Trim off ends from snow peas and pull strings, if necessary. In large saucepan, heat olive oil over medium heat. Add shallots, snow peas, and mushrooms.
2. Stir-fry for 3–5 minutes or until vegetables are crisp-tender. Stir in vinegar and lemon juice, then remove from heat and serve immediately.

Nutrition Info:
- Info Per Serving: Calories:133.38; Fat: 7.22g ;Saturated fat:1.02 g;Sodium:9.84 mg

White Bean, Sausage, And Escarole Soup

Servings: 6
Cooking Time: X

Ingredients:
- ¼ cup water
- 6 ounces Italian sweet turkey sausage
- 2 tablespoons olive oil
- 4 cloves garlic, minced
- 2 onions, chopped
- 2 (14-ounce) cans no-salt diced tomatoes, undrained
- 2 cups Beans for Soup , thawed
- 3 cups Low-Sodium Beef Broth
- 2 cups water
- 6 cups chopped escarole
- 1 teaspoon dried oregano
- 1 bunch parsley, chopped
- 1/3 cup grated Parmesan cheese

Directions:
1. Place sausage in soup pot over medium heat. Add ¼ cup water and bring to a simmer. Simmer sausage, turning occasionally, until water evaporates. Then cook sausage, turning frequently, until browned. Remove sausage from pot and discard drippings; do not wash pot. Cut sausage into ½" slices.
2. Add olive oil to pot and add garlic and onion. Cook and stir until tender, about 5 minutes. Add tomatoes and stir. Add beans to pot along with broth, water, escarole, and oregano. Simmer for 15–25 minutes until escarole is tender.
3. Add sausage and parsley to soup and simmer for 5 minutes. Serve each soup bowl with a sprinkling of Parmesan cheese.

Nutrition Info:
- Info Per Serving: Calories:282.43 ; Fat:8.20 g ;Saturated fat:1.46 g ;Sodium: 267.96 mg

Crunchy Cabbage And Carrot Salad

Servings: 5
Cooking Time: 15 Minutes

Ingredients:
- 3 cups shredded purple cabbage
- 1 cup carrots cut into thin matchsticks
- 1 cup diced cauliflower
- ½ cup slivered almonds
- ⅓ cup Honey-Garlic Sauce

Directions:
1. In a medium bowl, combine the cabbage, carrots, cauliflower, almonds, and the Honey-Garlic Sauce. Serve immediately.

Nutrition Info:
- Info Per Serving: Calories: 135 ; Fat: 8 g ;Saturated fat: 0g ;Sodium: 241 mg

Spicy Lentil

Servings: 4
Cooking Time: 20 Min

Ingredients:
- 2 cups cooked quinoa
- 1 cup low-sodium canned lentils, rinsed and drained
- 1 English cucumber, diced
- ½ jalapeño pepper, chopped
- ½ spring onion, thinly sliced
- ½ medium red bell pepper, finely chopped
- 1 lemon, juiced, and zested
- 1 tbsp. organic honey
- 1 tbsp. parsley, chopped
- Plastic wrap
- 2 tbsp. pine nuts, roasted and chopped for garnish

Directions:
1. In a large-sized mixing bowl, add the quinoa, lentils, cucumber, jalapeño, spring onion, and red bell pepper, mix until well incorporated.
2. Add the lemon juice, lemon zest, honey, and chopped parsley and mix well.
3. Cover the bowl with plastic wrap and chill the quinoa salad for 30 minutes in the refrigerator.
4. Serve topped with pine nuts.

Nutrition Info:

- Info Per Serving: Calories: 392 ; Fat: 5g ;Saturated fat: 1g ;Sodium:9 mg

Watermelon, Edamame, And Radish Salad

Servings: X
Cooking Time: X

Ingredients:
- 4 cups diced watermelon
- 2 cups shelled edamame
- 4 radishes, quartered
- 2 cups kale, torn into bite-size pieces
- ¼ cup Lemon-Cilantro Vinaigrette or store-bought balsamic vinaigrette
- ½ cup crumbled fat-free feta cheese, for garnish
- ¼ cup roasted, unsalted pumpkin seeds, for garnish

Directions:
1. In a medium bowl, add the watermelon, edamame, radishes, and kale.
2. Add the dressing and toss to coat.
3. Serve topped with feta and pumpkin seeds.

Nutrition Info:
- Info Per Serving: Calories: 514 ; Fat: 24 g ;Saturated fat: 3 g ;Sodium: 400 mg

Chili, Garlic, And Onion Kale Chips

Servings: 5
Cooking Time: 20 Minutes

Ingredients:
- 5 cups kale
- 1 tablespoon olive oil
- 1 teaspoon garlic powder
- 1 teaspoon chili powder
- ½ teaspoon onion powder

Directions:
1. Preheat the oven to 300°F. Line two baking sheets with parchment paper.
2. Wash and dry the kale thoroughly.
3. Remove the large stem from the kale leaves, then tear them into chip-size pieces.
4. In a large bowl, toss the kale with the olive oil, garlic powder, chili powder, and onion powder. Use your hands to massage the spiced oil thoroughly into each piece of kale.
5. Evenly distribute the kale in a single layer on the prepared baking sheets. Bake until the kale is crisp

and slightly brown, about 20 minutes. Watch the last 5 minutes of cooking carefully as kale burns easily. Enjoy immediately.

Nutrition Info:
• Info Per Serving: Calories: 36; Fat: 3 g ;Saturated fat: 0 g ;Sodium: 53 mg

Lemony Bulgur, Lentil, And Cucumber Salad

Servings: X
Cooking Time: X

Ingredients:
• 2 cups cooked bulgur
• 1 cup low-sodium canned lentils, rinsed and drained
• 1 English cucumber, diced
• ½ jalapeño pepper, chopped
• ½ scallion, white and green parts, thinly sliced
• ½ red bell pepper, finely chopped
• Juice and zest of 1 lemon
• 1 tablespoon granulated sugar
• 1 tablespoon chopped fresh cilantro
• 2 tablespoons chopped roasted peanuts, for garnish

Directions:
1. In a large bowl, toss together the bulgur, lentils, cucumber, jalapeño, scallion, and bell pepper until well mixed.
2. Add the lemon juice, lemon zest, sugar, and cilantro and toss to coat.
3. Cover the bowl and let the salad chill for 30 minutes in the refrigerator.
4. Serve topped with chopped peanuts.

Nutrition Info:
• Info Per Serving: Calories: 392; Fat: 5g ;Saturated fat:1g ;Sodium: 9 mg

Black Bean Soup

Servings: 5
Cooking Time: 25 Minutes

Ingredients:
• 1 tablespoon olive oil
• 1 cup chopped carrots
• 1 white onion, chopped
• 1 tablespoon minced garlic
• Pinch sea salt
• Pinch freshly ground black pepper
• 4 cups water

• 2 (19-ounce) cans low-sodium black beans, drained and rinsed
• ⅓ cup fresh cilantro, chopped

Directions:
1. In a large stockpot, heat the olive oil over high heat. Add the carrots, onion, garlic, salt, and pepper and cook for 3 minutes until fragrant.
2. Add the water and black beans and bring the soup to a boil. Reduce the heat to medium and simmer until the beans are soft, about 20 minutes.
3. Working in batches, carefully transfer the soup to a blender (or use a handheld immersion blender) and blend until smooth.
4. Top with cilantro and serve immediately.

Nutrition Info:
• Info Per Serving: Calories: 182; Fat: 3g ;Saturated fat: 1g ;Sodium: 51 mg

Baby Peas With Water Chestnuts

Servings: 4
Cooking Time: X

Ingredients:
• 1 tablespoon olive oil
• 2 shallots, minced
• 1 (8-ounce) can sliced water chestnuts, drained
• 2 cups frozen baby peas
• ¼ cup nonfat light cream
• 2 tablespoons grated Parmesan cheese

Directions:
1. In medium saucepan, heat olive oil over medium heat. Add shallots; cook for 1–2 minutes until fragrant. Add water chestnuts and peas; cook and stir until hot.
2. Add cream; bring to a simmer. Cook for 2 minutes, then add Parmesan, stir, and serve immediately.

Nutrition Info:
• Info Per Serving: Calories: 141.42; Fat: 4.79 g ;Saturated fat:1.19 g;Sodium:155.70 mg

Creamy Chicken And Corn Soup

Servings: 5
Cooking Time: 10 Minutes

Ingredients:
- 5¼ cups water, plus 2 tablespoons, divided
- 3 (14-ounce) cans low-sodium cream-style corn
- ½ pound skinless, boneless chicken breast, thinly sliced
- 1 cup liquid egg whites
- 3 tablespoons diced scallions, both green and white parts
- 1 teaspoon cornstarch
- Sea salt
- Freshly ground black pepper

Directions:
1. In a large stockpot, bring 5¼ cups of water to a boil over high heat.
2. Stir in the corn and return to a boil. Add the chicken and boil for 5 minutes.
3. Add the egg whites and scallions, reduce the heat to medium, and simmer for 5 minutes, until the egg whites turn opaque.
4. In a small bowl, mix the cornstarch with the remaining 2 tablespoons of water, then add it to the soup and stir until the soup thickens, about 1 or 2 minutes.
5. Season with salt and pepper and serve immediately.

Nutrition Info:
- Info Per Serving: Calories: 254 ; Fat: 2 g ;Saturated fat: 0g ;Sodium: 140 mg

Crab Edamame Salad

Servings: 4
Cooking Time: X

Ingredients:
- ¼ cup olive oil, divided
- 6 shallots, peeled and minced
- 2 tablespoons white-wine vinegar
- 2 tablespoons Dijon mustard
- ¼ teaspoon crushed red pepper flakes
- 2 tablespoons chopped flat-leaf parsley
- 2 (8-ounce) packages frozen surimi, thawed
- 1 (12-ounce) package frozen edamame
- 4 cups red leaf lettuce, torn
- 2 cups curly endive, torn

Directions:

1. In small saucepan, heat 1 tablespoon olive oil over medium heat. Add shallots; cook and stir until tender, about 3–4 minutes. Remove from heat and pour into serving bowl.
2. Add remaining olive oil, vinegar, mustard, pepper flakes, and parsley and blend with wire whisk until mixed.
3. Tear thawed surimi into bite-sized pieces and add to mustard mixture. Cook edamame as directed on package, drain, and add to mustard mixture. Toss gently to coat.
4. Add lettuce and endive and toss; serve immediately. You can refrigerate the surimi mixture up to 4 hours before serving; toss with lettuce and endive just before serving.

Nutrition Info:
- Info Per Serving: Calories:387.36; Fat:20.40g ;Saturated fat:2.75 g;Sodium: 273.14 mg

Curried Cauliflower Stew

Servings: 4
Cooking Time: 15 Minutes

Ingredients:
- 1 tablespoon olive oil
- 2 shallots, minced
- 1 tablespoon curry powder
- 2 cloves garlic, minced
- 2 carrots, sliced
- 1 head cauliflower, cut into florets and chopped
- ⅛ teaspoon white pepper
- 3 cups low-sodium vegetable broth
- 1 (14-ounce) can no-salt-added diced tomatoes, undrained
- 1 (15-ounce) can no-salt-added cannellini beans, rinsed and drained
- ½ cup chopped fresh flat-leaf parsley

Directions:
1. Heat the olive oil in a large saucepan over medium heat. Add the shallots, curry powder, and garlic, and cook and stir for 1 minute.
2. Add the carrots, cauliflower florets, white pepper, vegetable broth, tomatoes, and beans, and bring to a boil over medium heat.
3. Reduce the heat, partially cover the pot, and simmer for 13 to 14 minutes or until the cauliflower is tender.
4. Using a potato masher, mash some of the soup in the pot so it thickens. Top with the fresh parsley and

serve.

Nutrition Info:
- Info Per Serving: Calories: 247 ; Fat: 5g ;Saturated fat: 1 g ;Sodium: 182 mg

Chicken And Rice Noodle Soup

Servings: 4
Cooking Time: 20 Minutes

Ingredients:
- 5 ounces (150 grams) dry rice noodles
- 1 tablespoon olive oil
- ½ white onion, finely chopped
- ½ pound boneless, skinless chicken breast, thinly sliced
- ⅓ cup Tangy Soy Sauce
- 4 cups water
- ⅓ cup chopped fresh cilantro
- Sea salt
- Freshly ground black pepper

Directions:
1. Fill a medium stockpot two-thirds full with water and bring it to a boil over high heat. Submerge the rice noodles in the boiling water for 5 to 10 minutes until soft, or according to package directions, then remove them from the water and set aside.
2. In a large stockpot, heat the olive oil over high heat and sauté the onion until translucent, about 3 minutes.
3. Add the chicken and Tangy Soy Sauce and sauté until the chicken is browned, about 5 minutes.
4. Add the water and bring it to a boil, then reduce the heat to medium, and simmer for 10 minutes.
5. Add the cooked rice noodles to the soup and cook for 3 minutes until fragrant.
6. Remove the soup from the heat. Add the cilantro and season with salt and pepper. Enjoy immediately.

Nutrition Info:
- Info Per Serving: Calories: 259 ; Fat: 1 g ;Saturated fat: 0g ;Sodium: 335 mg

Vegetable-barley Stew

Servings: 8
Cooking Time: X

Ingredients:
- ¼ pound beef round steak
- 2 tablespoons flour
- 1 teaspoon paprika
- 2 tablespoons olive oil
- 2 onions, chopped
- 4 cups Low-Sodium Beef Broth , divided
- 4 carrots, thickly sliced
- 3 potatoes, cubed
- 1 (8-ounce) package sliced mushrooms
- 3 cups water
- 1 teaspoon dried marjoram leaves
- 1 bay leaf
- ¼ teaspoon salt
- ¼ teaspoon pepper
- ¼ cup hulled barley

Directions:
1. Trim beef and cut into 1" pieces. Sprinkle with flour and paprika and toss to coat. In large skillet, heat olive oil over medium heat. Add beef; brown beef, stirring occasionally, for about 5–6 minutes. Remove to 4- to 5-quart slow cooker.
2. Add onions to skillet along with ½ cup beef broth. Bring to a boil, then simmer, scraping the bottom of the skillet, for 3–4 minutes. Add to slow cooker along with all remaining ingredients.
3. Cover and cook on low for 8–9 hours, or until barley and vegetables are tender. Stir, remove bay leaf, and serve immediately.

Nutrition Info:
- Info Per Serving: Calories:295.45 ; Fat: 9.45 g;Saturated fat:2.59 g;Sodium:250.21 mg

Chicken Soup With Fall Vegetables

Servings: X
Cooking Time: 35 Minutes

Ingredients:
- 1 teaspoon olive oil
- 2 celery stalks, thinly sliced
- 2 carrots, diced
- 2 parsnips, diced
- ¼ sweet onion, peeled and chopped
- 1 teaspoon minced garlic
- 4 cups low-sodium chicken broth
- 1 cup diced sweet potato
- 1 cup diced cooked chicken breast
- ½ teaspoon chopped fresh thyme
- 1 cup small broccoli florets
- Sea salt
- Freshly ground black pepper

Directions:
1. In a medium saucepan, warm the oil over medium-high heat.
2. Add the celery, carrots, parsnips, onions, and garlic and sauté until softened, 7 to 8 minutes.
3. Stir in the broth, sweet potato, chicken, and thyme and bring the soup to a boil.
4. Reduce the heat to low and simmer for 20 minutes.
5. Add the broccoli and simmer until all the vegetables are tender, about 5 minutes.
6. Season with salt and pepper and serve.

Nutrition Info:
- Info Per Serving: Calories: 309 ; Fat: 5 g ;Saturated fat: 1 g ;Sodium: 239 mg

Cheese Polenta

Servings: 6
Cooking Time: X

Ingredients:
- ¼ teaspoon salt
- 3 cups water
- 1 cup skim milk
- 1¼ cups yellow cornmeal
- 1 tablespoon butter or plant sterol margarine
- ¼ cup grated Parmesan cheese
- ¼ cup shredded Havarti cheese
- ½ teaspoon crushed red pepper flakes

Directions:
1. In large saucepan, combine salt and water and bring to a boil. In small bowl, combine milk with cornmeal and mix until smooth.
2. Slowly add the cornmeal mixture to the boiling water, stirring constantly with a wire whisk. Cook over medium-low heat, stirring constantly, until polenta is very thick, about 5–10 minutes. Stir in butter, cheeses, and red pepper flakes. Serve immediately.

Nutrition Info:
- Info Per Serving: Calories: 171.53; Fat: 4.91g ;Saturated fat: 2.85 g;Sodium: 204.96 mg

Low Cholesterol
Cookbook

SAUCES, DRESS-INGS, AND STAPLES

Sauces, Dressings, And Staples

Avocado Dressing

Servings: 8
Cooking Time: 15 Minutes

Ingredients:
- 1 avocado, peeled and cubed
- ⅔ cup plain nonfat Greek yogurt
- ¼ cup buttermilk
- 2 tablespoons fresh lemon juice
- 1 tablespoon honey
- Pinch salt
- 2 tablespoons chopped fresh chives
- ½ cup chopped cherry tomatoes

Directions:
1. In a blender or food processor, combine the avocado, yogurt, buttermilk, lemon juice, honey, salt, and chives, and blend or process until smooth. Stir in the tomatoes.
2. You may need to add more buttermilk or lemon juice to achieve a pourable consistency.
3. This dressing can be stored by putting it into a small dish, then pouring about 2 teaspoons lemon juice on top. Cover the dressing by pressing plastic wrap directly onto the surface. Refrigerate for up to 1 day.

Nutrition Info:
- Info Per Serving: Calories:55 ; Fat: 3g ;Saturated fat: 1g ;Sodium: 30mg

Oregano-thyme Sauce

Servings: 5
Cooking Time: X

Ingredients:
- 2 tablespoons balsamic vinegar
- 1 tablespoon dried oregano
- 1 tablespoon dried thyme
- 1 tablespoon minced garlic
- ½ teaspoon salt

Directions:
1. In a small bowl, mix the vinegar, oregano, thyme, garlic, and salt until well blended. Use immediately

Nutrition Info:
- Info Per Serving: Calories: 10 ; Fat: 0 g ;Saturated fat: 0 g ;Sodium: 235 mg

Sweet Salad Dressing

Servings: 5
Cooking Time: X

Ingredients:
- ¼ cup low-sodium Worcestershire sauce (or ¼ cup Worcestershire sauce)
- 2 tablespoons minced garlic
- 1½ tablespoons honey
- 2 teaspoons onion powder
- ½ teaspoon freshly ground black pepper

Directions:
1. In a small bowl, mix the Worcestershire sauce, garlic, honey, onion powder, and pepper until well blended. Use immediately.

Nutrition Info:
- Info Per Serving: Calories: 39 ; Fat: 0g ;Saturated fat: 0g ;Sodium: 136mg

Double Tomato Sauce

Servings: 3
Cooking Time: 35 Minutes

Ingredients:
- 1 teaspoon olive oil
- ½ sweet onion, chopped
- 2 teaspoons minced garlic
- 1 (28-ounce) can low-sodium diced tomatoes with their juices
- ½ cup chopped sun-dried tomatoes
- Pinch red pepper flakes
- 2 tablespoons chopped fresh basil
- 2 tablespoons chopped fresh parsley
- Sea salt
- Freshly ground black pepper
- Whole-grain pasta or zucchini noodles, for serving (optional)

Directions:
1. In a large saucepan, warm the olive oil over medium-high heat.
2. Add the onions and garlic and sauté until softened,

about 3 minutes.

3. Stir in the tomatoes, sun-dried tomatoes, and red pepper flakes and bring the sauce to a simmer.

4. Reduce the heat and simmer for 20 to 25 minutes.

5. Stir in the basil and parsley and simmer for 5 more minutes.

6. Season with salt and pepper.

7. Serve over whole-grain pasta or zucchini noodles.

Nutrition Info:

*   Info Per Serving: Calories:94 ; Fat: 1 g ;Saturated fat: 0 g ;Sodium: 243mg

Spicy Peanut Sauce

Servings: 8
Cooking Time: 15 Minutes

Ingredients:

*   ½ cup powdered peanut butter (see Ingredient Tip)
*   2 tablespoons reduced-fat peanut butter
*   ⅓ cup plain nonfat Greek yogurt
*   2 tablespoons fresh lime juice
*   2 teaspoons low-sodium soy sauce
*   1 scallion, chopped
*   1 clove garlic, minced
*   1 jalapeño pepper, seeded and minced
*   ⅛ teaspoon red pepper flakes

Directions:

1. In a blender or food processor, combine powdered peanut butter, reduced-fat peanut butter, yogurt, lime juice, soy sauce, scallion, garlic, jalapeño pepper, and red pepper flakes, and blend or process until smooth.

2. Serve immediately or store in an airtight glass container and refrigerate for up to 3 days. You can thin this sauce with more lime juice if necessary.

Nutrition Info:

*   Info Per Serving: Calories: 60 ; Fat: 3 g ;Saturated fat: 0 g ;Sodium: 88 mg

Green Sauce

Servings: 4
Cooking Time: 15 Minutes

Ingredients:

*   1 cup watercress
*   ½ cup frozen baby peas, thawed
*   ¼ cup chopped fresh cilantro leaves
*   2 scallions, chopped
*   3 tablespoons silken tofu
*   2 tablespoons fresh lime juice
*   1 tablespoon green olive slices
*   1 teaspoon grated fresh lime zest
*   Pinch salt
*   Pinch white pepper

Directions:

1. In a food processor or blender, combine the watercress, peas, cilantro, scallions, tofu, lime juice, olives, lime zest, salt, and white pepper, and process or blend until smooth.

2. This sauce can be used immediately, or you can store it in an airtight glass container in the refrigerator up to four days.

Nutrition Info:

*   Info Per Serving: Calories: 27 ; Fat: 1 g ;Saturated fat: 0 g ;Sodium: 65 mg

Mango, Peach, And Tomato Pico De Gallo

Servings: 4
Cooking Time: 15 Minutes

Ingredients:

*   1 mango, peeled and cubed (see Ingredient Tip)
*   1 peach, peeled and chopped (see Ingredient Tip)
*   1 beefsteak tomato, cored and chopped
*   1 cup yellow or red cherry tomatoes, chopped
*   2 scallions, chopped
*   1 jalapeño pepper, seeded and minced
*   2 tablespoons fresh lemon juice
*   1 teaspoon fresh grated lemon zest
*   Pinch salt
*   ⅛ teaspoon red pepper flakes

Directions:

1. In a medium bowl, combine the mango, peach, tomato, scallions, jalapeño pepper, lemon juice, lemon zest, salt, and red pepper flakes, and mix well.

2. Serve immediately or store in an airtight glass container in the refrigerator for up to 2 days.

Nutrition Info:

*   Info Per Serving: Calories: 80 ; Fat: 1 g ;Saturated fat: 0 g ;Sodium: 48 mg

Silken Fruited Tofu Cream

Servings: 4
Cooking Time: 15 Minutes

Ingredients:
- 1 cup silken tofu
- ⅓ cup fresh raspberries
- 2 tablespoons orange-pineapple juice
- 1 tablespoon fresh lemon juice
- ½ teaspoon vanilla extract
- ⅛ teaspoon ground cinnamon
- Pinch salt

Directions:
1. In a blender or food processor, combine the tofu, raspberries, orange-pineapple juice, lemon juice, vanilla, cinnamon, and salt. Blend or process until smooth.
2. You can use this cream immediately or store it in an airtight glass container in the refrigerator for up to 2 days.

Nutrition Info:
- Info Per Serving: Calories: 49 ; Fat: 2 g ;Saturated fat: 0 g ;Sodium: 23 mg

Tofu-horseradish Sauce

Servings: X
Cooking Time: X

Ingredients:
- ¼ cup silken tofu
- 1 tablespoon prepared horseradish
- 1 tablespoon minced scallion, white part only
- 1 tablespoon chopped fresh parsley
- ½ teaspoon minced garlic
- Sea salt
- Freshly ground black pepper

Directions:
1. In a small bowl, stir together the tofu, horseradish, scallions, parsley, and garlic until well mixed.
2. Season with salt and pepper.
3. Serve immediately.

Nutrition Info:
- Info Per Serving: Calories: 20 ; Fat: 0 g ;Saturated fat: 0 g ;Sodium: 50 mg

Mustard Berry Vinaigrette

Servings: 8
Cooking Time: 10 Minutes

Ingredients:
- 3 tablespoons low-sodium yellow mustard
- ½ cup fresh raspberries
- ½ cup sliced fresh strawberries
- 2 tablespoons raspberry vinegar
- 2 teaspoons agave nectar
- Pinch salt

Directions:
1. In a blender or food processor, combine the mustard, raspberries, strawberries, raspberry vinegar, agave nectar, and salt, and blend or process until smooth. You can also combine the ingredients in a bowl and mash them with the back of a fork.
2. Store the vinaigrette in an airtight glass container in the refrigerator for up to 3 days.

Nutrition Info:
- Info Per Serving: Calories: 27 ; Fat: 1 g ;Saturated fat: 0 g ;Sodium: 65 mg

Chimichurri Rub

Servings: ½
Cooking Time: X

Ingredients:
- 2 tablespoons dried parsley
- 2 tablespoons dried basil
- 1 tablespoon hot paprika
- 1 tablespoon dried oregano
- 2 teaspoons garlic powder
- 1 teaspoon dried thyme
- 1 teaspoon onion powder
- ½ teaspoon freshly ground black pepper
- ¼ teaspoon sea salt
- Pinch red pepper flakes

Directions:
1. In a small bowl, whisk together the parsley, basil, paprika, oregano, garlic powder, thyme, onion powder, pepper, salt, and red pepper flakes until well blended.
2. Transfer to an airtight container to store.

Nutrition Info:
- Info Per Serving: Calories: 18 ; Fat: 0 g ;Saturated fat: 0 g ;Sodium: 90 mg

Smoky Barbecue Rub

Servings: ½
Cooking Time: X

Ingredients:
- 2 tablespoons smoked paprika
- 2 tablespoons brown sugar
- 1 tablespoon chili powder
- 1 tablespoon garlic powder
- 2 teaspoons onion powder
- 2 teaspoons celery salt
- 1 teaspoon ground cumin
- ½ teaspoon sea salt
- ½ teaspoon dried oregano

Directions:
1. In a small bowl, whisk together the paprika, sugar, chili powder, garlic powder, onion powder, celery salt, cumin, salt, and oregano until well blended.
2. Transfer to an airtight container to store.

Nutrition Info:
- Info Per Serving: Calories: 23 ; Fat: 1 g ;Saturated fat: 0 g ;Sodium: 113 mg

Tasty Tomato Sauce

Servings: 5
Cooking Time: 5 Minutes

Ingredients:
- 6 tablespoons low-sodium ketchup
- 2 tablespoons minced garlic
- 1½ tablespoons honey
- 1 tablespoon vinegar
- ½ teaspoon freshly ground black pepper

Directions:
1. In a small bowl, mix the ketchup, garlic, honey, vinegar, and pepper until well blended. Use immediately.

Nutrition Info:
- Info Per Serving: Calories: 46 ; Fat: 0g ;Saturated fat: 0g ;Sodium: 5 mg

Spicy Honey Sauce

Servings: 5
Cooking Time: X

Ingredients:
- 2 tablespoons vegetable oil
- 1½ tablespoons honey
- 1 tablespoon minced garlic
- 1 tablespoon chili powder
- ½ teaspoon salt

Directions:
1. In a small bowl, mix the vegetable oil, honey, garlic, chili powder, and salt until well blended. Use immediately.

Nutrition Info:
- Info Per Serving: Calories: 78 ; Fat: 6 g ;Saturated fat: 0 g ;Sodium: 279 mg

Tzatziki

Servings: 4
Cooking Time: X

Ingredients:
- 1¼ cups plain low-fat Greek yogurt
- 1 cucumber, peeled, seeded, and diced
- 2 tablespoons fresh lime juice
- ½ teaspoon grated fresh lime zest
- 2 cloves garlic, minced
- Pinch salt
- ⅛ teaspoon white pepper
- 1 tablespoon minced fresh dill
- 1 tablespoon minced fresh mint
- 2 teaspoons olive oil

Directions:
1. In a medium bowl, combine the yogurt, cucumber, lime juice, lime zest, garlic, salt, white pepper, dill, and mint.
2. Transfer the mixture to a serving bowl. Drizzle with the olive oil.
3. Serve immediately or store in an airtight glass container and refrigerate for up to 2 days

Nutrition Info:
- Info Per Serving: Calories: 100 ; Fat: 4 g ;Saturated fat: 1 g ;Sodium: 56 mg

Lemon-garlic Sauce

Servings: 5
Cooking Time: X

Ingredients:

- ¼ cup freshly squeezed lemon juice
- 2 tablespoons olive oil
- 1 tablespoon minced garlic
- 1 tablespoon dried oregano
- ½ teaspoon salt

Directions:

1. In a small bowl, mix the lemon juice, olive oil, garlic, oregano, and salt until well blended. Use immediately.

Nutrition Info:

- Info Per Serving: Calories: 55 ; Fat: 5 g ;Saturated fat: 1 g ;Sodium: 233 mg

Buttermilk-herb Dressing

Servings: ¾
Cooking Time: X

Ingredients:

- ½ cup buttermilk
- ¼ cup silken tofu
- 2 tablespoons minced scallion, white part only
- 1 tablespoon chopped fresh parsley
- 1 tablespoon chopped fresh thyme
- 1 teaspoon chopped fresh dill
- Sea salt
- Freshly ground black pepper

Directions:

1. In a medium bowl, whisk together the buttermilk, tofu, scallions, parsley, thyme, and dill until well blended.
2. Season with salt and pepper.

Nutrition Info:

- Info Per Serving: Calories: 17 ; Fat: 0 g ;Saturated fat: 0 g ;Sodium: 35 mg

Sweet Potato And Navy Bean Hummus

Servings: X
Cooking Time: X

Ingredients:

- 1 cup mashed cooked sweet potato
- 1 cup low-sodium canned navy beans, rinsed and drained
- 2 tablespoons tahini
- 2 tablespoons olive oil
- Juice of 1 lime
- ½ teaspoon minced garlic
- ¼ teaspoon ground cumin
- Sea salt
- Chopped fresh cilantro, for garnish
- Pita bread, baked tortilla crisps, or veggies, for serving

Directions:

1. In a food processor or blender, add the sweet potato, beans, tahini, olive oil, lime juice, garlic, and cumin and purée until very smooth, scraping down the sides at least once.
2. Season with salt, top with cilantro, and serve with pita bread, baked tortilla crisps, or veggies.

Nutrition Info:

- Info Per Serving: Calories: 396 ; Fat: 23 g ;Saturated fat: 3 g ;Sodium: 78 mg

Zesty Citrus Kefir Dressing

Servings: 8
Cooking Time: 15 Minutes

Ingredients:

- ⅔ cup kefir
- 2 tablespoons honey
- 2 tablespoons low-sodium yellow mustard
- 2 tablespoons fresh lemon juice
- ½ teaspoon fresh lemon zest
- 1 tablespoon fresh orange juice
- ½ teaspoon fresh orange zest
- 1 teaspoon olive oil
- Pinch salt

Directions:

1. In a blender or food processor, combine the kefir, honey, mustard, lemon juice and zest, orange juice and zest, olive oil, and salt. Blend or process until smooth.
2. You can serve this dressing immediately, or store it in an airtight container in the refrigerator for up to 3 days.

Nutrition Info:

- Info Per Serving: Calories: 37 ; Fat: 1 g ;Saturated fat: 0 g ;Sodium: 43 mg

Fresh Lime Salsa

Servings: 5
Cooking Time: X

Ingredients:
- 3 tomatoes, coarsely chopped
- ¼ cup chopped white onion
- ¼ cup chopped fresh cilantro
- 1 tablespoon minced garlic
- 1 tablespoon freshly squeezed lime juice
- Sea salt

Directions:
1. In a blender, place the tomatoes, onion, cilantro, garlic, and lime juice and blend until smooth. Season with salt and use immediately.

Nutrition Info:
- Info Per Serving: Calories: 20; Fat: 0 g ;Saturated fat: 0 g ;Sodium: 36 mg

Spinach And Walnut Pesto

Servings: 5
Cooking Time: X

Ingredients:
- 2 cups spinach
- ½ cup chopped walnuts
- ½ cup olive oil
- 2 tablespoons minced garlic
- ½ teaspoon salt

Directions:
1. In a blender, place the spinach, walnuts, olive oil, garlic, and salt and blend until smooth. Use immediately.

Nutrition Info:
- Info Per Serving: Calories: 275 ; Fat: 29 g ;Saturated fat: 4g ;Sodium: 243 mg

Simple Dijon And Honey Vinaigrette

Servings: ⅓
Cooking Time: X

Ingredients:
- 3 tablespoons olive oil
- 1½ tablespoons apple cider vinegar
- 1 tablespoon honey
- 2 teaspoons Dijon mustard
- Freshly ground black pepper

Directions:
1. In a small bowl, whisk together the oil, vinegar, honey, and mustard until emulsified.
2. Season with pepper and serve.

Nutrition Info:
- Info Per Serving: Calories: 145 ; Fat: 14 g ;Saturated fat: 2 g ;Sodium: 38 mg

Chimichurri Sauce

Servings: 8
Cooking Time: 15 Minutes

Ingredients:
- 1 shallot, chopped
- 1 garlic clove, chopped
- ½ cup fresh flat-leaf parsley
- ½ cup fresh cilantro leaves
- 3 tablespoons fresh basil leaves
- 2 tablespoons fresh lemon juice
- 2 tablespoons low-sodium vegetable broth
- Pinch salt
- ⅛ teaspoon red pepper flakes

Directions:
1. In a blender or food processor, add the shallot, garlic, parsley, cilantro, basil, lemon juice, vegetable broth, salt, and red pepper flakes, and process until the herbs are in tiny pieces and the mixture is well-combined.
2. Serve immediately or store in an airtight glass container in the refrigerator up to 2 days. Stir the sauce before serving.

Nutrition Info:
- Info Per Serving: Calories: 5 ; Fat: 0 g ;Saturated fat: 0 g ;Sodium: 3 mg

FISH AND SEAFOOD

Fish And Seafood

Creamy Tuna Sandwich

Servings: 2
Cooking Time: 10 Min

Ingredients:

- 1 (5 oz) can water-packed tuna, drained
- 1 ripe avocado, pitted, peeled, and mashed
- 2 spring onions, finely chopped
- ½ lemon, juiced
- 2 tbsp. avocado oil
- Pinch red pepper flakes
- ¼ tsp Himalayan pink salt
- ¼ tsp ground black pepper
- 4 whole-wheat bread slices

Directions:

1. In a small-sized mixing bowl, add the tuna, avocado, spring onions, lemon juice, avocado oil, red pepper flakes, salt and pepper, mix to combine.
2. Spoon equal amounts of the tuna and avocado mixture on one side of the 4 slice bread and top with the other slice. Repeat with the last 2 slices of bread.

Nutrition Info:

- Info Per Serving: Calories: 518; Fat:32 g ;Saturated fat: 5 g ;Sodium: 567mg

Salmon With Spicy Mixed Beans

Servings: 4
Cooking Time: 20 Minutes

Ingredients:

- 2 teaspoons olive oil, divided
- 4 (4-ounce) salmon fillets
- Pinch salt
- ⅛ teaspoon black pepper
- 1 onion, diced
- 3 cloves peeled garlic, minced
- 1 jalapeño pepper, seeded and minced
- 1 (16-ounce) can low-sodium mixed beans, rinsed and drained
- 2 tablespoons low-fat plain Greek yogurt
- 2 tablespoons minced fresh cilantro

Directions:

1. Put 1 teaspoon of the olive oil in a large skillet and heat over medium heat.

2. Sprinkle the salmon fillets with the salt and pepper and add to the skillet, skin side down.
3. Cook for 5 minutes, then flip the fillets with a spatula and cook for another 3 to 4 minutes or until the salmon flakes when tested with a fork. Remove the fish to a clean warm plate, and cover with an aluminum foil tent to keep warm.
4. Add the remaining 1 teaspoon of the olive oil to the skillet. Add the onion, garlic, and jalapeño pepper; cook, stirring frequently, for 3 minutes.
5. Add the beans and mash with a fork until desired consistency.
6. Remove the pan from the heat, add the yogurt, and stir until combined.
7. Pile the beans onto a serving platter, top with the fish, and sprinkle with the cilantro. Serve immediately.

Nutrition Info:

- Info Per Serving: Calories: 293 ; Fat: 10 g ;Saturated fat: 2 g;Sodium: 345 mg

Poached Chilean Sea Bass With Pears

Servings: 4
Cooking Time: X

Ingredients:

- ½ cup dry white wine
- ¼ cup water
- 2 bay leaves
- 1/8 teaspoon salt
- ½ teaspoon Tabasco sauce
- 1 lemon, thinly sliced
- 4 (4–5) ounce sea bass steaks or fillets
- 2 firm pears, cored and cut in half
- 1 tablespoon butter

Directions:

1. In large skillet, combine wine, water, bay leaves, salt, Tabasco, and lemon slices. Bring to a simmer over medium heat.
2. Add fish and pears. Reduce heat to low and poach for 9–12 minutes or until fish flakes when tested with a fork.
3. Remove fish and pears to serving platter. Remove bay leaves from poaching liquid and increase heat to high. Boil for 3–5 minutes or until liquid is reduced

and syrupy. Swirl in butter and pour over fish and pears; serve immediately.

Nutrition Info:
- Info Per Serving: Calories:235.38 ; Fat: 5.81 g ;Saturated fat: 2.55 g ;Sodium:194.06 mg

Grilled Scallops With Gremolata

Servings: 4
Cooking Time: 6 Minutes

Ingredients:
- 2 scallions, cut into pieces
- ¾ cup packed fresh flat-leaf parsley
- ¼ cup packed fresh basil leaves
- 1 teaspoon lemon zest
- 3 tablespoons fresh lemon juice
- 1 tablespoon olive oil
- 20 sea scallops
- 2 teaspoons butter, melted
- Pinch salt
- ⅛ teaspoon lemon pepper

Directions:
1. Prepare and preheat the grill to medium-high. Make sure the grill rack is clean.
2. Meanwhile, make the gremolata. In a blender or food processor, combine the scallions, parsley, basil, lemon zest, lemon juice, and olive oil. Blend or process until the herbs are finely chopped. Pour into a small bowl and set aside.
3. Put the scallops on a plate. If the scallops have a small tough muscle attached to them, remove and discard it. Brush the melted butter over the scallops. Sprinkle with the salt and the lemon pepper.
4. Place the scallops in a grill basket, if you have one. If not, place a sheet of heavy-duty foil on the grill, punch some holes in it, and arrange the scallops evenly across it.
5. Grill the scallops for 2 to 3 minutes per side, turning once, until opaque. Drizzle with the gremolata and serve.

Nutrition Info:
- Info Per Serving: Calories: 190 ; Fat: 7 g ;Saturated fat: 2 g;Sodium: 336 mg

Sesame-pepper Salmon Kabobs

Servings: 4
Cooking Time: X

Ingredients:

- 1 pound salmon steak
- 2 tablespoons olive oil, divided
- ¼ cup sesame seeds
- 1 teaspoon pepper
- 1 red bell pepper
- 1 yellow bell pepper
- 1 red onion
- 8 cremini mushrooms
- 1/8 teaspoon salt

Directions:
1. Prepare and preheat grill. Cut salmon steak into 1" pieces, discarding skin and bones. Brush salmon with half of the olive oil.
2. In small bowl, combine sesame seeds and pepper and mix. Press all sides of salmon cubes into the sesame seed mixture.
3. Slice bell peppers into 1" slices and cut red onion into 8 wedges; trim mushroom stems and leave caps whole. Skewer coated salmon pieces, peppers, onion, and mushrooms on metal skewers. Brush vegetables with remaining olive oil and sprinkle with salt.
4. Grill 6" from medium coals, turning once during cooking time, until the sesame seeds are very brown and toasted and fish is just done, about 6–8 minutes. Serve immediately.

Nutrition Info:
- Info Per Serving: Calories:319.33 ; Fat:20.26 g ;Saturated fat: 3.67 g ;Sodium:141.88 mg

Vietnamese Fish And Noodle Bowl

Servings: 3
Cooking Time: 15 Minutes

Ingredients:
- ¾ pound grouper fillets, cut into 1-inch pieces
- 1 tablespoon cornstarch
- ⅛ teaspoon cayenne pepper
- 2 teaspoons fish sauce
- 1 tablespoon rice wine vinegar
- 1 teaspoon sugar
- 2 tablespoons fresh lemon juice
- 1 teaspoon olive oil
- ¼ cup minced daikon radish
- 3 cloves garlic, minced
- 4 ounces whole-wheat spaghetti, broken in half
- 1½ cups low-sodium vegetable broth
- 2 tablespoons chopped peanuts
- 2 tablespoons minced fresh cilantro
- 2 tablespoons minced fresh basil

Directions:

1. In a medium bowl, toss the grouper with the cornstarch and cayenne pepper and set aside.
2. In a small bowl, combine the fish sauce, rice wine vinegar, sugar, and lemon juice, and stir to mix well.
3. In a large skillet, heat the olive oil over medium heat. Add the daikon and garlic and cook for 1 minute, stirring constantly.
4. Add the fish to the skillet; sauté for 2 to 3 minutes, stirring frequently, until the fish browns lightly.
5. Remove the fish mixture to a large bowl and set aside.
6. Add the spaghetti and vegetable broth to the skillet, and stir. Bring to a simmer over high heat and cook for 7 to 8 minutes or until the pasta is al dente.
7. Return the fish and radish mixture to the skillet along with the fish sauce mixture, peanuts, cilantro, and basil. Toss for 1 minute, then serve immediately in bowls.

Nutrition Info:

• Info Per Serving: Calories: 324 ; Fat: 6 g ;Saturated fat: 1 g;Sodium: 439 mg

Seared Scallops With Fruit

Servings: 3–4
Cooking Time: X

Ingredients:

• 1 pound sea scallops Pinch salt
• 1/8 teaspoon white pepper
• 1 tablespoon olive oil
• 1 tablespoon butter or margarine
• ¼ cup dry white wine
• 2 peaches, sliced
• 1 cup blueberries
• 1 tablespoon lime juice

Directions:

1. Rinse scallops and pat dry. Sprinkle with salt and pepper and set aside.
2. In large skillet, heat olive oil and butter over medium-high heat. Add the scallops and don't move them for 3 minutes. Carefully check to see if the scallops are deep golden brown. If they are, turn and cook for 1–2 minutes on the second side.
3. Remove scallops to serving plate. Add peaches to skillet and brown quickly on one side, about 2 minutes. Turn peaches and add wine to skillet; bring to a boil. Remove from heat and add blueberries. Pour over scallops, sprinkle with lime juice, and serve im-

mediately.

Nutrition Info:

• Info Per Serving: Calories: 207.89; Fat: 7.36 g ;Saturated fat:2.40 g ;Sodium: 242.16 mg

Scallops On Skewers With Lemon

Servings: 4
Cooking Time: X

Ingredients:

• 2 tablespoons lemon juice
• 1 teaspoon grated lemon zest
• 2 teaspoons sesame oil
• 2 tablespoons chili sauce
• 1/8 teaspoon cayenne pepper
• 1 pound sea scallops
• 4 strips low-sodium bacon

Directions:

1. Prepare and preheat grill or broiler. In medium bowl, combine lemon juice, zest, sesame oil, chili sauce, and cayenne pepper and mix well. Add scallops and toss to coat. Let stand for 15 minutes.
2. Make skewers with the scallops and bacon. Thread a skewer through one end of the bacon, then add a scallop. Curve the bacon around the scallop and thread onto the skewer so it surrounds the scallop halfway. Repeat with 3 to 4 more scallops and the bacon slice.
3. Repeat with remaining scallops and bacon. Grill or broil 6" from heat source for 3–5 minutes per side, until bacon is crisp and scallops are cooked and opaque. Serve immediately.

Nutrition Info:

• Info Per Serving: Calories:173.65 ; Fat:6.48 g ;Saturated fat: 1.51 g;Sodium:266.64 mg

Roasted Shrimp And Veggies

Servings: 4
Cooking Time: 20 Minutes

Ingredients:

• 1 cup sliced cremini mushrooms
• 2 medium chopped Yukon Gold potatoes, rinsed, unpeeled
• 2 cups broccoli florets
• 3 cloves garlic, sliced
• 1 cup sliced fresh green beans
• 1 cup cauliflower florets
• 2 tablespoons fresh lemon juice

- 2 tablespoons low-sodium vegetable broth
- 1 teaspoon olive oil
- 1 teaspoon dried thyme
- ½ teaspoon dried oregano
- Pinch salt
- ⅛ teaspoon black pepper
- ½ pound medium shrimp, peeled and deveined

Directions:

1. Preheat the oven to 400°F.
2. In a large baking pan, combine the mushrooms, potatoes, broccoli, garlic, green beans, and cauliflower, and toss to coat.
3. In a small bowl, combine the lemon juice, broth, olive oil, thyme, oregano, salt, and pepper and mix well. Drizzle over the vegetables
4. Roast for 15 minutes, then stir.
5. Add the shrimp and distribute evenly.
6. Roast for another 5 minutes or until the shrimp curl and turn pink. Serve immediately.

Nutrition Info:

- Info Per Serving: Calories:192 ; Fat: 3 g ;Saturated fat: 0 g;Sodium: 116 mg

Baked Halibut In Mustard Sauce

Servings: 4
Cooking Time: X

Ingredients:

- 1 pound halibut fillet Pinch of salt
- 1/8 teaspoon white pepper
- 1 tablespoon lemon juice
- 1 teaspoon orange zest
- 2 tablespoons butter or margarine, melted
- ¼ cup skim milk
- 2 tablespoons Dijon mustard
- 1 slice Honey-Wheat Sesame Bread , crumbled

Directions:

1. Preheat oven to 400ºF. Spray a 1-quart baking dish with nonstick cooking spray. Cut fish into serving-size pieces and sprinkle with salt, pepper, and lemon juice.
2. In small bowl, combine melted butter, milk, and mustard, and whisk until blended. Stir in the breadcrumbs. Pour this sauce over the fish.
3. Bake for 20–25 minutes, or until fish flakes when tested with fork and sauce is bubbling. Serve immediately.

Nutrition Info:

- Info Per Serving: Calories: 219.84 ; Fat:9.38 g ;Satu-

rated fat: 4.30 g ;Sodium: 244.95 mg

Cajun-rubbed Fish

Servings: 4
Cooking Time: X

Ingredients:

- ½ teaspoon black pepper
- ¼ teaspoon cayenne pepper
- ½ teaspoon lemon zest
- ½ teaspoon dried dill weed
- 1/8 teaspoon salt
- 1 tablespoon brown sugar
- 4 (5-ounce) swordfish steaks

Directions:

1. Prepare and preheat grill. In small bowl, combine pepper, cayenne pepper, lemon zest, dill weed, salt, and brown sugar and mix well. Sprinkle onto both sides of the swordfish steaks and rub in. Set aside for 30 minutes.
2. Brush grill with oil. Add swordfish; cook without moving for 4 minutes. Then carefully turn steaks and cook for 2–4 minutes on second side until fish just flakes when tested with fork. Serve immediately.

Nutrition Info:

- Info Per Serving: Calories: 233.57 ; Fat:7.31 g ;Saturated fat: 2.00 g ;Sodium: 237.08 mg

Poached Fish With Tomatoes And Capers

Servings: 4
Cooking Time: X

Ingredients:

- 2 tablespoons olive oil
- ½ cup chopped red onion
- 2 cloves garlic, minced
- 1 cup chopped fresh tomatoes
- 2 tablespoons no-salt tomato paste
- ¼ cup dry white wine
- 2 tablespoons capers, rinsed
- 4 (4-ounce) white fish fillets
- ¼ cup chopped parsley

Directions:

1. In large skillet, heat olive oil over medium heat. Add onion and garlic; cook and stir until tender, about 5 minutes. Add tomatoes, tomato paste, and wine and bring to a simmer; simmer for 5 minutes, stirring fre-

quently.

2. Add capers to sauce and stir, then arrange fillets on top of sauce. Spoon sauce over fish. Reduce heat to low, cover, and poach for 7–10 minutes, or until fish flakes when tested with fork. Sprinkle with parsley and serve immediately.

Nutrition Info:

- Info Per Serving: Calories: 191.05 ; Fat:7.70 g ;Saturated fat: 1.13 g ;Sodium: 199.73 mg

Tuna Patties

Servings: 6
Cooking Time: 10 Min

Ingredients:

- 12 oz canned, water-packed tuna, drained
- 4 tbsp. almond flour
- 1 large free-range egg white
- 1 tbsp. brown onion, finely chopped
- ½ lemon, juiced
- ½ tsp parsley, finely chopped
- Pinch red pepper flakes
- Pinch Himalayan pink salt
- Pinch ground black pepper
- Cooking spray

Directions:

1. In a medium-sized mixing bowl, add the tuna, almond flour, egg white, onions, lemon juice, parsley, red pepper flakes, salt, and pepper, mix to combine.
2. Mold the tuna mixture into 6 equal patties.
3. Place the tuna cakes on a plate and chill for 1 hour in the refrigerator until firm.
4. Spray a large, heavy-bottom pan with cooking spray and place it over medium-high heat.
5. Add the tuna cakes to the pan and cook for 5 minutes per side, turning once, until browned and heated through. Serve.

Nutrition Info:

- Info Per Serving: Calories: 243 ; Fat: 6 g ;Saturated fat: 0 g ;Sodium: 558 mg

Crispy Mixed Nut Fish Fillets

Servings: 4
Cooking Time: 15 Minutes

Ingredients:

- 4 (6-ounce) white fish fillets, such as red snapper or cod
- 2 tablespoons low-sodium yellow mustard

- 2 tablespoons nonfat plain Greek yogurt
- 2 tablespoons low-fat buttermilk
- 1 teaspoon dried Italian herb seasoning
- ⅛ teaspoon white pepper
- ¼ cup hazelnut flour
- 2 tablespoons almond flour
- 2 tablespoons ground almonds
- 2 tablespoons ground hazelnuts

Directions:

1. Preheat the oven to 400°F. Line a baking sheet with a fine wire rack and set aside.
2. Pat the fish dry and place on a plate.
3. In a shallow bowl, combine the mustard, yogurt, buttermilk, Italian seasoning, and white pepper.
4. On a plate, combine the hazelnut flour and almond flour, and add the ground almonds, the ground hazelnuts, and mix well.
5. Coat the fish with the mustard mixture, then coat with the nut mixture. Place on the prepared baking sheet.
6. Bake the fish for 12 to 17 minutes, until it flakes when tested with a fork. Serve immediately.

Nutrition Info:

- Info Per Serving: Calories: 256 ; Fat: 9 g ;Saturated fat: 1 g;Sodium: 206 mg

Halibut Parcels

Servings: 4
Cooking Time: 15 Min

Ingredients:

- Aluminum foil
- 4 cups kale, stems removed and shredded
- 2 cups button mushrooms, sliced
- 4 (4 oz) halibut fillets
- ½ tsp seafood seasoning
- ½ tsp fine sea salt
- ¼ tsp ground black pepper
- ¼ cup spring onion, chopped
- 2 tbsp. olive oil

Directions:

1. Heat the oven to 425°F gas mark 7.
2. Prepare the aluminum foil by tearing them into squares, big enough for the fillets and vegetables.
3. Place 1 cup of kale and ½ cup of mushroom onto each foil square.
4. Place the halibut fillet on top of each parcel. Season with seafood seasoning, salt and pepper.
5. Sprinkle the spring onion over this and drizzle with

olive oil.

6. Fold the foil to seal in the halibut and vegetables.

7. Place on a baking sheet and bake for 15 minutes. Remove from the oven and carefully unfold the parcels.

Nutrition Info:

• Info Per Serving: Calories:155 ; Fat: 7 g ;Saturated fat: 1 g ;Sodium: 435 mg

Catalán Salmon Tacos

Servings: 4
Cooking Time: 20 Minutes

Ingredients:

• 1 teaspoon olive oil
• 1 (6-ounce) salmon fillet
• 1 teaspoon chili powder
• ½ teaspoon dried oregano leaves
• ⅛ teaspoon black pepper
• 1 small onion, diced
• 2 cloves peeled garlic, minced
• 1 (16-ounce) can low-sodium white beans, rinsed and drained
• 1 tomato, chopped
• 1 cup torn fresh Swiss chard leaves
• 2 tablespoons pine nuts
• 4 corn tortillas, heated

Directions:

1. Add the olive oil to a large nonstick skillet and place over medium heat. Rub the salmon fillet with the chili powder, oregano, and pepper.

2. Add the salmon to the pan, skin side down. Cook for 3 minutes, then turn and cook for 5 minutes longer, or until the fish flakes when tested with a fork. Remove the salmon from the pan, flake, and set aside.

3. Add the onion and garlic to the pan and cook for 2 to 3 minutes, stirring frequently, until softened.

4. Add the beans and mash some of them into the onions. Cook for 1 minute, stirring occasionally.

5. Add the tomato and Swiss chard and cook for another 1 to 2 minutes until the greens start to wilt. Add the pine nuts to the mixture.

6. Make the tacos by adding the bean mixture and the salmon to the corn tortillas, and fold them in half. Serve immediately.

Nutrition Info:

• Info Per Serving: Calories: 296 ; Fat: 8 g ;Saturated fat: 1 g;Sodium: 63 mg

Flounder Fillet Bake

Servings: 4
Cooking Time: 15 Min

Ingredients:

• Aluminum foil
• 4 (4 oz) flounder fillets
• 2 tbsp. avocado oil
• 1 tsp ground thyme
• ½ tsp Himalayan pink salt
• ¼ tsp ground black pepper
• 1 lime, cut into wedges
• 2 tbsp. cilantro, finely chopped

Directions:

1. Heat the oven to 400°F gas mark 6. Line a baking sheet with aluminum foil.

2. Place the flounder fillets on the baking sheet and drizzle with avocado oil.

3. Season both sides of the fillets with thyme, salt pepper.

4. Bake for 6 to 8 minutes, flip, and bake for a further 5 minutes, or until cooked through. Remove from the oven.

5. Serve the flounder fillets with a lime wedge and sprinkle with cilantro.

Nutrition Info:

• Info Per Serving: Calories: 164 ; Fat: 8 g ;Saturated fat: 1 g ;Sodium: 369 mg

Red Snapper Scampi

Servings: 4
Cooking Time: 20 Minutes

Ingredients:

• 2 teaspoons olive oil
• 4 cloves garlic, minced
• ¼ cup fresh lemon juice
• ¼ cup white wine or fish stock
• 1 teaspoon fresh lemon zest
• Pinch salt
• ⅛ teaspoon lemon pepper
• 4 (6-ounce) red snapper fillets
• 2 scallions, minced
• 3 tablespoons minced flat-leaf fresh parsley

Directions:

1. Preheat the oven to 400°F. Line a baking pan with parchment paper.

2. In a small bowl, combine the olive oil, garlic, lemon juice, white wine, lemon zest, salt, and lemon pepper.

3. Arrange the fillets skin side down, if the skin is attached, on the prepared baking pan. Pour the lemon juice mixture over the fillets.

4. Roast for 15 to 20 minutes, or until the fish flakes when tested with a fork.

5. Serve the fish with the pan drippings, sprinkled with the scallions and parsley.

Nutrition Info:
• Info Per Serving: Calories: 212 ; Fat: 5 g ;Saturated fat: 1 g;Sodium: 112 mg

Sesame-crusted Mahi Mahi

Servings: 4
Cooking Time: X

Ingredients:
• 4 (4-ounce) mahi mahi or sole fillets
• 2 tablespoons Dijon mustard
• 1 tablespoon low-fat sour cream
• ½ cup sesame seeds
• 2 tablespoons olive oil
• 1 lemon, cut into wedges

Directions:
1. Rinse fillets and pat dry. In small bowl, combine mustard and sour cream and mix well. Spread this mixture on all sides of fish. Roll in sesame seeds to coat.

2. Heat olive oil in large skillet over medium heat. Pan-fry fish, turning once, for 5–8 minutes or until fish flakes when tested with fork and sesame seeds are toasted. Serve immediately with lemon wedges.

Nutrition Info:
• Info Per Serving: Calories: 282.75; Fat: 17.17 g ;Saturated fat:2.84 g ;Sodium: 209.54 mg

Broiled Swordfish

Servings: 4
Cooking Time: X

Ingredients:
• 1 tablespoon olive oil
• 2 tablespoons dry white wine
• 1 teaspoon lemon zest
• ¼ teaspoon salt
• 1/8 teaspoon white pepper
• 1 teaspoon dried dill weed
• 1¼ pounds swordfish steaks
• 4 ½-inch-thick tomato slices

Directions:
1. Preheat broiler. In small bowl, combine oil, wine, zest, salt, pepper, and dill weed and whisk to blend.

2. Place steaks on broiler pan. Brush steaks with oil mixture. Broil 6" from heat for 4 minutes. Turn fish and brush with remaining oil mixture. Top with tomatoes. Return to broiler and broil for 4–6 minutes or until fish flakes when tested with fork.

Nutrition Info:
• Info Per Serving: Calories: 210.97 ; Fat:9.10 g ;Saturated fat: 2.03 g ;Sodium:273.91 mg

Halibut Burgers

Servings: 4
Cooking Time: 35 Min

Ingredients:
• Aluminum foil
• 1 lb. halibut fillets
• ½ tsp Himalayan pink salt, divided
• ¼ tsp ground black pepper
• ½ cup whole wheat breadcrumbs
• 1 large free-range egg
• 1 tbsp. garlic, crushed
• ½ tsp dried dill
• 2 tbsp. avocado oil
• 4 whole wheat buns

Directions:
1. Heat the oven to 400°F gas mark 6. Line a baking sheet with aluminum foil.

2. Place the halibut fillets on the baking sheet and season with ¼ tsp salt and pepper. Bake for 15 to 20 minutes, or until the halibut flakes with a fork. Remove from the oven.

3. Transfer the flesh into a medium-sized mixing bowl, removing any bones.

4. Add the breadcrumbs, egg, garlic, dill and the remaining ¼ tsp salt, mix to combine.

5. Mold the fish mixture into 4 patties.

6. Heat the avocado oil in a large heavy bottom pan over medium heat.

7. Gently place the halibut patties in the pan. Fry for 5 to 6 minutes, until browned, flip, and cook for 3 to 5 minutes, remove from the heat.

8. Place 1 fish patty on each of the 4 buns and serve.

Nutrition Info:
• Info Per Serving: Calories: 294 ; Fat: 16 g ;Saturated fat: 3 g ;Sodium: 458 mg

Shrimp Stir-fry

Servings: 2
Cooking Time: 15 Min

Ingredients:
- 12 oz zucchini spirals
- 2 tsp low-sodium tamari sauce
- 2 tsp apple cider vinegar
- 1 tsp ginger, peeled and grated
- 1 tsp garlic, crushed
- 1 tsp organic honey
- 2 tsp sesame oil
- 6 oz shrimp, peeled and deveined
- 2 cups napa cabbage, shredded
- 1 medium green bell pepper, thinly sliced
- 1 spring onion, thinly sliced
- 1 tbsp. toasted sesame seeds, for garnish

Directions:
1. Cook the zucchini according to the package directions. Drain and run under cold water to stop the cooking process. Transfer the zucchini to a medium-sized mixing bowl and set aside.
2. In a small-sized mixing bowl, add the tamari sauce, apple cider vinegar, ginger, garlic, and honey, mix to combine, and set aside.
3. Warm the sesame oil in a medium-sized, heavy-bottom pan over medium-high heat. Add the shrimp and fry for 5 minutes until cooked through.
4. Add the napa cabbage, green bell pepper, and spring onion and fry for 4 minutes until the vegetables are tender. Add the tamari sauce mixture and the zucchini, toss to coat, heat for 1 minute.
5. Serve into bowls and top with sesame seeds.

Nutrition Info:
- Info Per Serving: Calories: 400 ; Fat: 8 g ;Saturated fat: 1 g ;Sodium: 347 mg

Northwest Salmon

Servings: 4
Cooking Time: X

Ingredients:
- 4 tablespoons olive oil, divided
- 5 juniper berries, crushed
- ½ cup chopped red onion
- 1 cup blueberries
- ½ cup chopped hazelnuts
- ¼ cup dry white wine
- 4 (5-ounce) salmon fillets Pinch salt
- 1/8 teaspoon white pepper
- 2 cups watercress

Directions:
1. Preheat grill or broiler. In small saucepan, heat 3 tablespoons of the olive oil. Add juniper berries and red onion; cook and stir for 3 minutes. Add blueberries, hazelnuts, and wine and bring to a simmer.
2. Meanwhile, sprinkle salmon with salt and pepper and brush with olive oil. Broil or grill 6" from heat until salmon flakes when tested with a fork. Place salmon on watercress and pour blueberry sauce over all; serve immediately.

Nutrition Info:
- Info Per Serving: Calories: 362.66; Fat:22.63 g ;Saturated fat:3.27 g ;Sodium: 105.81 mg

POULTRY

Iron Packed Turkey

Servings: 2
Cooking Time: 30 Min

Ingredients:
- 2 (3 oz) turkey breasts, boneless and skinless
- Himalayan pink salt
- Ground black pepper
- 3 tsp avocado oil, divided
- 1 ½ cups spinach, roughly chopped
- 1 ½ cups kale, roughly chopped
- 1 ½ cups Swiss chard, roughly chopped
- 1 ½ cups collard greens, roughly chopped
- 1 tsp garlic crushed

Directions:
1. Preheat the oven to 400°F gas mark 6.
2. Season the turkey breasts with salt and pepper to taste.
3. Heat 1 tsp of avocado oil in a large cast-iron frying pan over medium-high heat.
4. Add the turkey breasts and cook for 5 minutes on each side until browned. Remove the turkey breasts and set them aside.
5. Add the remaining 2 tsp of avocado oil to the pan and fry the spinach, kale, Swiss chard, collard greens and garlic for 3 minutes until they are slightly wilted.
6. Season the mixed greens with salt and pepper to taste, place the turkey breasts on the greens.
7. Place the cast iron frying pan in the oven and bake for 15 minutes until the turkey breasts are cooked through.
8. Serve warm

Nutrition Info:
- Info Per Serving: Calories: 113 ; Fat: 2 g ;Saturated fat: 0 g ;Sodium: 128 mg

Lime Turkey Skewers

Servings: 4
Cooking Time: 15 Min

Ingredients:
- 1 lb. boneless, skinless turkey breasts, cut into chunks
- 1 lime, juiced
- 2 tbsp. avocado oil, plus 1 tbsp.
- 2 tbsp. garlic, minced
- 1 tsp dried thyme
- 1 tsp dried dill
- ½ tsp fine sea salt
- ¼ tsp ground black pepper

Directions:
1. In a medium-sized mixing bowl, add the turkey breasts, lime juice, avocado oil, garlic, thyme, dill, salt and pepper, mix to combine. Rest for 30 minutes in the fridge.
2. Thread the marinated turkey chunks onto 8 skewers.
3. Heat 1 tbsp. of avocado oil in a heavy-bottom pan over medium-high heat.
4. Place the skewers gently in the pan and fry for 5 to 7 minutes, flip, and cook for 5 to 8 minutes, or until the turkey is cooked through and no longer pink inside. Remove from the heat and serve.

Nutrition Info:
- Info Per Serving: Calories: 205 ; Fat: 10 g ;Saturated fat: 2 g ;Sodium: 343 mg

Moroccan Chicken

Servings: 4
Cooking Time: 15 Minutes

Ingredients:
- 3 (4-ounce) boneless, skinless chicken thighs, cubed
- 1 teaspoon smoked paprika
- ½ teaspoon ground cinnamon
- ½ teaspoon ground cumin
- ⅛ teaspoon ground ginger
- 1 cup low-sodium chicken broth
- 2 tablespoons fresh lemon juice
- 1 tablespoon cornstarch
- 1 teaspoon olive oil
- 1 onion, chopped
- 3 cloves garlic, minced
- 2 cups sugar snap peas
- 1 cup shredded carrots

Directions:
1. Put the cubed chicken in a medium bowl. Sprinkle with the paprika, cinnamon, cumin, and ginger, and

work the spices into the meat. Set aside.

2. In a small bowl, combine the chicken broth, lemon juice, and cornstarch and mix well. Set aside.

3. Heat the olive oil in a large nonstick skillet over medium-high heat. Add the chicken thighs, and sauté for 5 minutes or until the chicken starts to brown. Remove the chicken from the pan and set aside.

4. Add the onion and garlic to the skillet, and sauté for 3 minutes.

5. Add the sugar snap peas and carrots to the skillet and sauté for 2 minutes.

6. Return the chicken to the skillet and stir. Add the chicken broth mixture, bring to a simmer, and turn down the heat to low. Simmer 3 to 4 minutes or until the sauce thickens, the vegetables are tender, and the chicken is cooked to 165°F on a meat thermometer. Serve hot.

Nutrition Info:

• Info Per Serving: Calories: 165 ; Fat : 5 g ;Saturated fat: 1 g ;Sodium: 112 mg

Italian Chicken Bake

Servings: 4
Cooking Time: 25 Min

Ingredients:

• 1 lb. chicken breasts, halved lengthwise into 4 pieces
• ½ tsp garlic powder
• ½ tsp fine sea salt
• ¼ tsp ground black pepper
• ¼ tsp Italian seasoning
• ½ cup basil, finely chopped
• 4 part-skim mozzarella cheese slices
• 2 large Roma tomatoes, finely chopped

Directions:

1. Heat the oven to 400°F gas mark 6.

2. Season the cut chicken breasts with garlic powder, salt, pepper and Italian seasoning.

3. Place the seasoned chicken breasts on a baking sheet. Bake for 18 to 22 minutes, or until the chicken breasts are cooked through. Remove from the oven and set it to broil on high.

4. Evenly place the basil, 1 mozzarella slice and tomatoes on each chicken breast.

5. Return the baking sheet to the oven and broil for 2 to 3 minutes, until the cheese has melted and browned.

6. Remove from the oven and serve hot.

Nutrition Info:

• Info Per Serving: Calories: 239 ; Fat: 9 g ;Saturated fat: 4 g ;Sodium: 524 mg

Asian Chicken Stir-fry

Servings: 4
Cooking Time: X

Ingredients:

• 2 (5-ounce) boneless, skinless chicken breasts
• ½ cup Low-Sodium Chicken Broth
• 1 tablespoon low-sodium soy sauce
• 1 tablespoon cornstarch
• 1 tablespoon sherry
• 2 tablespoons peanut oil
• 1 onion, sliced
• 3 cloves garlic, minced
• 1 tablespoon grated ginger root
• 1 cup snow peas
• ½ cup canned sliced water chestnuts, drained
• 1 yellow summer squash, sliced
• ¼ cup chopped unsalted peanuts

Directions:

1. Cut chicken into strips and set aside. In small bowl, combine chicken broth, soy sauce, cornstarch, and sherry and set aside.

2. In large skillet or wok, heat peanut oil over medium-high heat. Add chicken; stir-fry until almost cooked, about 3–4 minutes. Remove to plate. Add onion, garlic, and ginger root to skillet; stir-fry for 4 minutes longer. Then add snow peas, water chestnuts, and squash; stir-fry for 2 minutes longer.

3. Stir chicken broth mixture and add to skillet along with chicken. Stir-fry for 3–4 minutes longer or until chicken is thoroughly cooked and sauce is thickened and bubbly. Sprinkle with peanuts and serve immediately.

Nutrition Info:

• Info Per Serving: Calories: 252.42; Fat: 12.42 g ;Saturated fat:2.06 g ;Sodium: 202.04 mg

Basil Chicken Meatballs

Servings: 20
Cooking Time: 10 Minutes

Ingredients:

- 1 egg white
- ⅓ cup gluten-free (or whole-wheat) bread crumbs
- ½ cup low-sodium chicken broth, divided
- 1 tablespoon fresh lemon juice
- 1 tablespoon freeze-dried chopped chives
- 3 tablespoons minced fresh basil leaves
- ⅛ teaspoon garlic powder
- Pinch salt
- Pinch black pepper
- ¾ pound ground white chicken breast meat

Directions:

1. In a medium bowl, combine the egg white, bread crumbs, 2 tablespoons of the chicken broth, lemon juice, chives, basil, garlic powder, salt, and pepper, and mix well.
2. Add the ground chicken and mix gently but thoroughly until combined.
3. Form into 20 meatballs, about 1 inch in diameter.
4. Heat the remaining 6 tablespoons of the chicken broth in a large nonstick skillet over medium-high heat.
5. Gently add the chicken meatballs in a single layer. Let cook for 5 minutes, then carefully turn and cook another 3 minutes.
6. Lower the heat as the broth reduces, and continue cooking the meatballs, gently shaking the pan occasionally, until the broth has mostly evaporated and the meatballs are browned and cooked to 165°F as tested with a meat thermometer, another 2 to 3 minutes.

Nutrition Info:

- Info Per Serving: Calories: 130 ; Fat : 3 g ;Saturated fat: 1 g ;Sodium: 162 mg

Nutty Coconut Chicken With Fruit Sauce

Servings: 4
Cooking Time: 15 Minutes

Ingredients:

- ¼ cup ground almonds
- ⅓ cup unsweetened flaked coconut
- ¼ cup coconut flour
- Pinch salt
- ⅛ teaspoon white pepper
- 1 egg white

- 1 (16-ounce) package chicken tenders
- 1 cup sliced strawberries
- 1 cup raspberries
- ⅓ cup unsweetened white grape juice
- 1 tablespoon lemon juice
- ½ teaspoon dried thyme leaves
- ⅓ cup dried cherries

Directions:

1. Preheat the oven to 400°F. Place a wire rack on a baking sheet.
2. In a shallow plate, combine the ground almonds, flaked coconut, coconut flour, salt, and white pepper, and mix well.
3. In a shallow bowl, beat the egg white just until foamy.
4. Dip the chicken tenders into the egg white, then into the almond mixture to coat. Place on the wire rack as you work.
5. Bake the chicken tenders for 14 to 16 minutes or until the chicken is cooked to 165°F when tested with a meat thermometer.
6. While the chicken is baking, in a food processor or blender, combine the strawberries, raspberries, grape juice, lemon juice, and thyme leaves and process or blend until smooth.
7. Pour the mixture into a small saucepan, and add the dried cherries. Bring to a simmer over medium heat. Simmer for 3 minutes, then remove the pan from the heat and set aside.
8. Serve the chicken with the warm fruit sauce.

Nutrition Info:

- Info Per Serving: Calories: 281 ; Fat : 8 g ;Saturated fat: 3 g ;Sodium: 124 mg

Mustard-roasted Almond Chicken Tenders

Servings: 4
Cooking Time: 15 Minutes

Ingredients:

- ¼ cup low-sodium yellow mustard
- 2 teaspoons yellow mustard seed
- ¼ teaspoon dry mustard
- ⅛ teaspoon garlic powder
- 1 egg white
- 2 tablespoons fresh lemon juice
- ¼ cup almond flour
- ¼ cup ground almonds
- 1 pound chicken tenders

Directions:

1. Preheat the oven to 400°F. Place a wire rack on a baking sheet.
2. In a shallow bowl, combine the yellow mustard, mustard seed, ground mustard, garlic powder, egg white, and lemon juice, and whisk well.
3. To a plate or shallow bowl, add the almond flour and ground almonds, and combine.
4. Dip the chicken tenders into the mustard-egg mixture, then into the almond mixture to coat. Place each tender on the rack on the baking pan as you work.
5. Bake the chicken for 12 to 15 minutes or until a meat thermometer registers 165°F. Serve immediately.

Nutrition Info:

• Info Per Serving: Calories: 166 ; Fat : 4 g ;Saturated fat: 0 g ;Sodium: 264 mg

Chicken Breasts With Mashed Beans

Servings: 6
Cooking Time: X

Ingredients:

• 3 tablespoons olive oil, divided
• 1 onion, chopped
• 3 cloves garlic, minced
• 1 (14-ounce) can low-sodium cannellini beans
• ½ cup chopped flat-leaf parsley
• ½ teaspoon dried oregano leaves
• 1 teaspoon dried basil leaves
• ¼ cup grated Parmesan cheese
• 3 tablespoons flour
• ¼ teaspoon white pepper
• 6 (4-ounce) boneless, skinless chicken breasts

Directions:

1. In medium saucepan, heat 1 tablespoon olive oil and add onion and garlic. Cook and stir until tender, about 5 minutes. Drain beans, rinse, and drain again.
2. Add to saucepan along with parsley, oregano, and basil. Cook until hot, stirring frequently, about 5 minutes. Using a potato masher, mash the bean mixture. Turn heat to very low.
3. On shallow plate, combine Parmesan, flour, and pepper and mix well. Coat chicken on both sides with cheese mixture. In large skillet, heat remaining 2 tablespoons olive oil over medium heat.
4. Add chicken to skillet; cook for 5 minutes without moving. Carefully turn chicken and cook for 4–6 minutes until thoroughly cooked. Serve with mashed

beans.

Nutrition Info:

• Info Per Serving: Calories:316.30; Fat:10.55 g ;Saturated fat:2.56 g;Sodium: 133.71 mg

Pineapple Curried Chicken

Servings: 4
Cooking Time: 15 Minutes

Ingredients:

• 3 (6-ounce) boneless, skinless chicken breasts, cubed
• 2 teaspoons curry powder
• 2 tablespoons cornstarch
• ⅛ teaspoon cayenne pepper
• 1 teaspoon olive oil
• 2 shallots, minced
• 3 cloves garlic, minced
• 1 (16-ounce) can pineapple chunks, drained, reserving juice
• 2 teaspoons yellow curry paste (optional)
• ⅓ cup reserved pineapple juice
• 1 tablespoon fresh lemon juice
• 3 tablespoons plain nonfat Greek yogurt

Directions:

1. In a medium bowl, toss the chicken breast cubes with the curry powder, cornstarch, and cayenne pepper, and set aside.
2. In a large nonstick skillet, heat the olive oil over medium heat.
3. Add the shallots and garlic, and cook for 2 minutes, stirring frequently.
4. Add the coated chicken cubes. Cook and stir for 5 to 6 minutes or until the chicken starts to brown.
5. Add the pineapple chunks, yellow curry paste (if using), reserved pineapple juice, and lemon juice to the skillet and bring to a simmer.
6. Simmer for 3 to 4 minutes or until the chicken is cooked to 165°F when tested with a meat thermometer. Stir in the yogurt and serve hot.

Nutrition Info:

• Info Per Serving: Calories: 260 ; Fat : 3 g ;Saturated fat: 1 g ;Sodium: 93 mg

Chicken Paillards With Mushrooms

Servings: 4
Cooking Time: X

Ingredients:
- 4 (3-ounce) chicken breasts
- 3 tablespoons flour
- 1/8 teaspoon salt
- 1/8 teaspoon cayenne pepper
- ½ teaspoon dried marjoram leaves
- 2 tablespoons olive oil
- 4 shallots, minced
- 1 cup sliced button mushrooms
- 1 cup sliced cremini mushrooms
- ½ cup Low-Sodium Chicken Broth
- ¼ cup dry white wine
- 1 teaspoon Worcestershire sauce
- 1 tablespoon cornstarch

Directions:

1. Place chicken breasts between two sheets of waxed paper and pound until ¼" thick. On shallow plate, combine flour, salt, pepper, and marjoram. Dredge chicken in flour mixture to coat.

2. In large skillet, heat olive oil over medium heat. Add chicken; sauté on first side for 3 minutes, then carefully turn and cook for 1 minute longer. Remove to platter and cover to keep warm.

3. Add shallots and mushrooms to skillet; cook and stir for 4–5 minutes until tender. Meanwhile, in small bowl combine broth, wine, Worcestershire sauce, and cornstarch, and mix well. Add to mushroom mixture and bring to a boil.

4. Return chicken to skillet; cook until chicken is hot and sauce bubbles and thickens. Serve immediately over brown rice, couscous, or pasta.

Nutrition Info:
- Info Per Serving: Calories:270.13; Fat:8.25g ;Saturated fat:1.71 g ;Sodium: 167.63 mg

"butter" Chicken

Servings: 4
Cooking Time: 12 Minutes

Ingredients:
- 4 (6-ounce) boneless, skinless chicken breasts, cubed
- 2 tablespoons fresh lemon juice
- 2 teaspoons curry powder
- 1 teaspoon chili powder
- ⅛ teaspoon black pepper
- 2 teaspoons olive oil
- 1 onion, chopped
- 4 cloves garlic, minced
- ½ cup low-fat coconut milk
- ½ cup low-fat plain Greek yogurt
- 2 tablespoons no-salt-added tomato paste
- 1 tablespoon cornstarch

Directions:

1. In a large bowl, combine the chicken with the lemon juice, curry powder, chili powder, and black pepper, and mix with your hands, rubbing the spices into the chicken. Set aside.

2. In a large nonstick skillet, heat the olive oil over medium heat.

3. Add the onion and garlic, and sauté for 4 to 5 minutes, until tender.

4. Add the chicken and sauté, stirring frequently, until the chicken starts to brown, about 4 minutes.

5. Meanwhile, in a small bowl, combine the coconut milk, yogurt, tomato paste, and cornstarch, and mix well with a whisk.

6. Add the coconut milk mixture to the skillet. Simmer 4 to 5 minutes or until the sauce is thickened and the chicken registers 165°F on a meat thermometer. Serve hot.

Nutrition Info:
- Info Per Serving: Calories: 308 ; Fat : 8 g ;Saturated fat: 3 g ;Sodium: 144 mg

Piri Piri Chicken

Servings: 4
Cooking Time: 15 Minutes

Ingredients:
- 3 (6-ounce) boneless, skinless chicken breasts, cubed
- 2 tablespoons lemon juice
- 1 teaspoon smoked paprika
- ½ teaspoon cayenne pepper
- Pinch salt
- 2 teaspoons chili powder
- 1 teaspoon olive oil
- 1 onion, chopped
- 4 cloves garlic, minced
- 1 red bell pepper, chopped
- 1 red chile pepper, such as chile de arbol, seeded and minced
- 2 tablespoons Piri Piri sauce

- 1 cup low-sodium chicken broth
- 1 tablespoon cornstarch

Directions:

1. Place the chicken breasts in a medium bowl and drizzle with the lemon juice.

2. Sprinkle the chicken with the smoked paprika, cayenne pepper, salt, and chili powder. Work the spices into the chicken with your hands and set aside.

3. In a large nonstick skillet, heat the olive oil over medium heat.

4. Add the chicken to the skillet. Cook, stirring frequently, until the chicken is lightly browned, about 4 minutes. Transfer the chicken to a clean plate.

5. Add the onion, garlic, red bell pepper, red chile pepper, and Piri Piri sauce to the skillet stir. Sauté 3 to 4 minutes or until the vegetables are crisp-tender. Return the chicken to the skillet.

6. In a small bowl, combine the chicken broth and cornstarch and mix with a whisk. Stir into the chicken mixture.

7. Simmer 3 to 4 minutes or until the chicken is cooked to 165°F when tested with a meat thermometer, and the sauce is thickened. Serve immediately.

Nutrition Info:

- Info Per Serving: Calories: 209 ; Fat : 5 g ;Saturated fat: 1 g ;Sodium: 210 mg

Turkey With Prunes

Servings: 6
Cooking Time: X

Ingredients:

- 3 tablespoons olive oil
- 1 onion, chopped
- 3 cloves garlic, minced
- 1 cup finely chopped pitted prunes
- 1/8 teaspoon salt
- 1/8 teaspoon pepper
- ½ cup chopped hazelnuts
- 6 (3-ounce) turkey cutlets
- 2 tablespoons flour
- ½ cup Low-Sodium Chicken Broth
- ¼ cup dry white wine
- ½ teaspoon dried thyme leaves
- 1 tablespoon lemon juice

Directions:

1. In small saucepan, heat 1 tablespoon olive oil over medium heat. Add onion and garlic; cook and stir until crisp-tender, about 4 minutes. Add prunes and sprinkle with salt and pepper. Cook for 3–4 minutes or until prunes begin to plump. Add nuts and remove from heat. Let cool for 20 minutes.

2. Arrange turkey cutlets on work surface. Divide prune mixture among the cutlets. Roll up, securing with kitchen twine or toothpicks. Dredge filled cutlets in flour.

3. Heat remaining 2 tablespoons olive oil in large skillet. Brown turkey, turning to cook evenly, for about 4–5 minutes. Then add broth, wine, and thyme leaves to skillet. Cover and braise cutlets for 6–8 minutes or until turkey is tender and thoroughly cooked. Add lemon juice and serve immediately.

Nutrition Info:

- Info Per Serving: Calories: 327.80; Fat: 15.34 g ;Saturated fat: 2.04 g;Sodium: 92.23 mg

Hawaiian Chicken Stir-fry

Servings: 4
Cooking Time: 10 Minutes

Ingredients:

- 1 (8-ounce) can crushed pineapple, undrained
- ⅓ cup water
- 2 tablespoons cornstarch
- 1 teaspoon brown sugar
- 1 teaspoon low-sodium tamari sauce
- ¼ teaspoon ground ginger
- ⅛ teaspoon cayenne pepper
- 2 tablespoons unsweetened shredded coconut
- 2 tablespoons chopped macadamia nuts
- 2 teaspoons olive oil
- 1 onion, chopped
- 1 red bell pepper, seeded and chopped
- 3 (6-ounce) boneless, skinless chicken breasts, cubed

Directions:

1. In a medium bowl, combine the pineapple, water, cornstarch, brown sugar, tamari, ginger, and cayenne pepper, and mix well. Set aside.

2. Place a large nonstick skillet or wok over medium heat. Add the coconut and macadamia nuts, and toast for 1 to 2 minutes, stirring constantly, until fragrant. Remove from the skillet and set aside.

3. Add the olive oil to the skillet and heat over medium-high heat. Add the onion and red bell pepper, and stir-fry for 2 to 3 minutes or until almost tender.

4. Add the chicken to the wok, and stir-fry for 3 to 4 minutes or until lightly browned.

5. Stir the sauce, add to the skillet, and stir fry for 1 to 2 minutes longer until the sauce thickens and the chicken registers at 165°F when tested with a meat thermometer.

6. Serve immediately, topped with the toasted coconut and macadamia nuts.

Nutrition Info:
- Info Per Serving: Calories: 301 ; Fat : 12 g ;Saturated fat: 4 g ;Sodium: 131 mg

Cold Chicken With Cherry Tomato Sauce

Servings: 3
Cooking Time: X

Ingredients:
- 2 teaspoons fresh thyme leaves
- ½ cup Low-Sodium Chicken Broth
- 12 ounces boneless, skinless chicken breasts
- 1 tablespoon olive oil
- 3 cloves garlic, minced
- 2 cups cherry tomatoes
- ½ cup no-salt tomato juice
- ½ cup chopped fresh basil
- ¼ cup low-fat sour cream
- 1/8 teaspoon white pepper

Directions:
1. In large saucepan, combine thyme and chicken broth; bring to a simmer over medium heat. Add chicken and reduce heat to low. Cover and poach for 7–9 minutes or until chicken is thoroughly cooked.

2. Place chicken in a casserole dish just large enough to hold the chicken. Pour poaching liquid over, then cover and refrigerate for at least 8 hours.

3. When ready to eat, heat olive oil in large skillet. Add garlic; cook and stir for 1 minute. Then stir in cherry tomatoes; cook and stir until the tomatoes pop, about 4–6 minutes. Add tomato juice, basil, sour cream, and pepper; stir, and heat briefly.

4. Slice the chicken and fan out on serving plate. Top with tomato mixture and serve immediately.

Nutrition Info:
- Info Per Serving: Calories: 227.58; Fat: 8.63 g   ;Saturated fat: 2.57 g ;Sodium: 198.32 mg

Chicken Poached In Tomato Sauce

Servings: 4
Cooking Time: X

Ingredients:
- 1 cup brown rice
- 2 cups water
- 2 tablespoons olive oil
- 1 onion, chopped
- 3 cloves garlic, minced
- 2 cups chopped plum tomatoes
- ½ teaspoon dried tarragon
- ¼ cup dry red wine
- 3 tablespoons no-salt tomato paste
- 1 cup Low-Sodium Chicken Broth
- 1/8 teaspoon salt
- 1/8 teaspoon pepper
- 3 (5-ounce) boneless, skinless chicken thighs, sliced

Directions:
1. In medium saucepan, combine rice and water and bring to a boil over high heat. Reduce heat to low, cover, and simmer for 30–40 minutes or until rice is tender.

2. Meanwhile, in large saucepan heat olive oil over medium heat. Add onion and garlic; cook and stir for 4 minutes until crisp-tender. Add tomatoes, tarragon, wine, tomato paste, chicken broth, salt, and pepper, and bring to a simmer, stirring frequently.

3. Add chicken and bring back to a simmer. Cover pan, reduce heat to low, and poach chicken for 15–20 minutes or until thoroughly cooked. Serve over hot cooked rice.

Nutrition Info:
- Info Per Serving: Calories: 285.33; Fat: 9.22g ;Saturated fat: 1.70 g;Sodium: 129.66 mg

Turkey Curry With Fruit

Servings: 6
Cooking Time: X

Ingredients:
- 6 (4-ounce) turkey cutlets
- 1 tablespoon flour
- 1 tablespoon plus
- 1 teaspoon curry powder, divided
- 1 tablespoon olive oil
- 2 pears, chopped
- 1 apple, chopped ½ cup raisins
- 1 tablespoon sugar

- 1/8 teaspoon salt
- 1/3 cup apricot jam

Directions:

1. Preheat oven to 350ºF. Spray a cookie sheet with sides with nonstick cooking spray. Arrange cutlets on prepared cookie sheet. In small bowl, combine flour, 1 tablespoon curry powder, and olive oil and mix well. Spread evenly over cutlets.

2. In medium bowl, combine pears, apple, raisins, sugar, salt, 1 teaspoon curry powder, and apricot jam, and mix well. Divide this mixture over the turkey cutlets.

3. Bake for 35–45 minutes or until turkey is thoroughly cooked and fruit is hot and caramelized. Serve immediately.

Nutrition Info:

- Info Per Serving: Calories: 371.52; Fat: 11.15 g ;Saturated fat: 2.80 g ;Sodium: 121.35 mg

Turkey Cutlets Parmesan

Servings: 6
Cooking Time: X

Ingredients:

- 1 egg white
- ¼ cup dry breadcrumbs
- 1/8 teaspoon pepper
- 4 tablespoons grated Parmesan cheese, divided
- 6 (4-ounce) turkey cutlets
- 2 tablespoons olive oil
- 1 (15-ounce) can no-salt tomato sauce
- 1 teaspoon dried Italian seasoning
- ½ cup finely shredded part-skim mozzarella cheese

Directions:

1. Preheat oven to 350ºF. Spray a 2-quart baking dish with nonstick cooking spray and set aside.

2. In shallow bowl, beat egg white until foamy. On plate, combine breadcrumbs, pepper, and 2 tablespoons Parmesan. Dip the turkey cutlets into the egg white, then into the breadcrumb mixture, turning to coat.

3. In large saucepan, heat olive oil over medium heat. Add turkey cutlets; brown on both sides, about 2–3 minutes per side. Place in prepared baking dish. Add tomato sauce and Italian seasoning to saucepan; bring to a boil.

4. Pour sauce over cutlets in baking pan and top with mozzarella cheese and remaining 2 tablespoons Parmesan. Bake for 25–35 minutes or until sauce bubbles

and cheese melts and begins to brown. Serve with pasta, if desired.

Nutrition Info:

- Info Per Serving: Calories: 275.49; Fat: 10.98 g ;Saturated fat:3.43 g ;Sodium: 229.86 mg

Sesame-crusted Chicken

Servings: 4
Cooking Time: X

Ingredients:

- 2 tablespoons low-sodium soy sauce
- 2 cloves garlic, minced
- 1 tablespoon grated ginger root
- 1 tablespoon brown sugar
- 1 teaspoon sesame oil
- 4 (4-ounce) boneless, skinless chicken breasts
- ½ cup sesame seeds
- 3 tablespoons olive oil
- 1 tablespoon butter

Directions:

1. In large food storage heavy-duty plastic bag, combine soy sauce, garlic, ginger root, brown sugar, and sesame oil and mix well. Add chicken; seal bag, and squish to coat chicken with marinade. Place in bowl and refrigerate for 8 hours.

2. When ready to eat, remove chicken from marinade; discard marinade. Dip chicken in sesame seeds to coat on all sides.

3. Heat olive oil and butter in large skillet over medium heat. Add chicken and cook for 5 minutes. Carefully turn chicken and cook for 3–6 minutes on second side or until chicken is thoroughly cooked and sesame seeds are toasted. Serve immediately.

Nutrition Info:

- Info Per Serving: Calories: 363.65; Fat: 20.83 g ;Saturated fat:4.15 g;Sodium: 250.28 mg

Tomatoes With Chicken Mousse

Servings: 4
Cooking Time: X

Ingredients:

- 1 cup diced cooked chicken
- ¼ cup minced red onion
- 1 tablespoon chopped fresh chives
- 1 tablespoon fresh rosemary, minced
- 1/3 cup low-fat yogurt
- ¼ cup low-fat mayonnaise

- 1 tablespoon lime juice
- ½ cup chopped celery
- 4 large ripe tomatoes

Directions:

1. In blender or food processor, combine all ingredients except celery and tomatoes. Blend or process until smooth. Stir in celery.

2. Cut the tops off the tomatoes and scoop out the insides, leaving a " shell. Turn upside down on paper towels and let drain for 10 minutes.

3. Fill tomatoes with the chicken mixture and top each with the tomato top. Cover and chill for 2–3 hours before serving.

Nutrition Info:

- Info Per Serving: Calories:169.29; Fat: 7.01 g ;Saturated fat:1.41 g ;Sodium: 167.31 mg

Chicken Breasts With Salsa

Servings: 4
Cooking Time: X

Ingredients:

- 2 tablespoons lime juice, divided
- 1 egg white
- 1 cup whole-grain cereal, crushed
- 1 teaspoon dried thyme leaves
- ¼ teaspoon pepper
- 4 (4-ounce) boneless, skinless chicken breasts
- 1 cup Super Spicy Salsa
- 1 jalapeño pepper, minced

Directions:

1. Preheat oven to 375ºF. Line a cookie sheet with a wire rack and set aside. In small bowl, combine 1 tablespoon lime juice and egg white; beat until frothy. On shallow plate, combine crushed cereal, thyme, and pepper.

2. Dip chicken into egg white mixture, then into cereal mixture to coat. Place on prepared cookie sheet. Bake for 20–25 minutes or until chicken is thoroughly cooked and coating is crisp.

3. Meanwhile, in small saucepan combine remaining 1 tablespoon lime juice, salsa, and jalapeño pepper. Heat through, stirring occasionally. Serve with chicken.

Nutrition Info:

- Info Per Serving: Calories: 264.05; Fat: 4.43 g ;Saturated fat:1.18 g ;Sodium: 146.85 mg

Cashew Chicken

Servings: 2
Cooking Time: 5 Min

Ingredients:

- 2 tsp olive oil
- 2 tsp garlic, minced, divided
- ½ cup red onion, chopped
- 8 oz ground chicken
- 1 tsp ginger, grated
- 3 tbsp. unsalted cashew butter
- 4 tbsp. water
- 6 large green leaf lettuce leaves
- ½ cup unsalted cashew nuts, roughly chopped

Directions:

1. Heat the olive oil in a medium-sized frying pan over medium heat. Add the 1 tsp garlic and onion, cook for 1 to 2 minutes, until translucent.

2. Add the chicken and separate using a fork. Continue mixing for 5 minutes until lightly golden and cooked through.

3. In a small-sized mixing bowl, add the ginger, remaining 1 tsp garlic, cashew butter, and water, mix to combine.

4. Add the cashew mixture to the ground chicken. Cook for 1 minute until all flavors have combined.

5. Divide the cashew chicken mixture into the lettuce cups and serve topped with the cashew nuts.

Nutrition Info:

- Info Per Serving: Calories: 414 ; Fat: 21 g ;Saturated fat: 4 g ;Sodium: 211 mg

PORK AND BEEF MAINS

Pork Tenderloin With Apples

Servings: 6
Cooking Time: X

Ingredients:
- 1½ pounds pork tenderloin
- 1/8 teaspoon salt
- 1/8 teaspoon pepper
- 2 tablespoons flour
- 2 tablespoons olive oil
- 1 onion, chopped
- 4 cloves garlic, minced
- 2 apples, thinly sliced
- ½ cup dry white wine
- 1 tablespoon chopped fresh rosemary

Directions:
1. Trim excess fat from pork and sprinkle with salt, pepper, and flour. Heat olive oil in large saucepan and brown pork on all sides, about 5 minutes total.
2. Add onion, garlic, apples, and wine to saucepan, and bring to a simmer. Reduce heat to low, cover, and simmer for 20 minutes. Add rosemary, uncover, and simmer for 5–10 minutes longer or until pork registers 155ºF. Let stand for 5 minutes off the heat, then serve.

Nutrition Info:
- Info Per Serving: Calories: 243.96 ; Fat:9.42 g ;Saturated fat: 2.34 g ;Sodium: 100.07 mg

Whole-wheat Spaghetti And Meatballs

Servings: 6–8
Cooking Time: X

Ingredients:
- 1 recipe Sirloin Meatballs in Sauce
- 1 (8-ounce) can no-salt tomato sauce
- ½ cup grated carrots
- 1 (16-ounce) package whole-wheat spaghetti
- ½ cup grated Parmesan cheese, divided

Directions:
1. Bring a large pot of water to a boil. Prepare the Sirloin Meatballs in Sauce, adding tomato sauce and grated carrots to the sauce. Simmer until meatballs are cooked.
2. Cook spaghetti in water according to package direc-tions or until almost al dente. Drain spaghetti, reserving ¼ cup cooking water. Add spaghetti to meatballs in sauce along with ¼ cup of the cheese. Simmer, stirring gently, for 5–6 minutes or until pasta is al dente, adding reserved cooking water if necessary for desired sauce consistency. Sprinkle with the remaining ¼ cup Parmesan cheese and serve immediately.

Nutrition Info:
- Info Per Serving: Calories: 386.78; Fat:12.34 g ;Saturated fat: 4.08 g ;Sodium: 444.23 mg

Pork Goulash

Servings: 4
Cooking Time: 15 Minutes

Ingredients:
- ½ pound lean ground pork
- 2 onions, chopped
- 8 ounces sliced button mushrooms
- 4 cloves garlic, minced
- 3 stalks celery, sliced
- ½ cup grated carrot
- 2 teaspoons smoked paprika
- Pinch salt
- ⅛ teaspoon white pepper
- 1 (14-ounce) can no-salt-added diced tomatoes
- 1 (8-ounce) can no-salt-added tomato sauce
- 2 tablespoons tomato paste
- ½ cup water
- 1 cup whole-wheat orzo

Directions:
1. In a large skillet over medium-high, sauté the pork, onions, mushrooms, garlic, celery, and carrot for 4 minutes, stirring to break up the pork, until the meat is almost cooked through.
2. Add the paprika, salt, white pepper, tomatoes, tomato sauce, tomato paste, and water, and bring to a simmer. Simmer for 1 minute.
3. Add the orzo to the skillet and stir, making sure that the pasta is covered by liquid. Simmer for 10 to 12 minutes or until the pasta is cooked al dente. Serve immediately.

Nutrition Info:
- Info Per Serving: Calories:299 ; Fat:7 g ;Saturated

fat: 2 g ;Sodium: 128 mg

Cowboy Steak With Chimichurri Sauce

Servings: 4–6
Cooking Time: X

Ingredients:
- 1 cup chopped parsley
- ¼ cup minced fresh oregano leaves
- ¼ cup extra-virgin olive oil
- 2 tablespoons lemon juice
- 3 tablespoons sherry vinegar
- 6 cloves garlic, minced
- 1/8 teaspoon salt
- ¼ teaspoon pepper
- 1 pound flank steak
- 2 tablespoons red wine
- 2 tablespoons olive oil

Directions:
1. In blender or food processor, combine parsley, oregano, olive oil, lemon juice, sherry vinegar, garlic, salt, and pepper; blend or process until smooth. Pour into small bowl, cover, and refrigerate until ready to use.
2. Pierce flank steak all over with a fork. Place in large heavy-duty zip-close freezer bag and add red wine and olive oil. Seal bag and squish to mix. Place in pan and refrigerate for 8–12 hours.
3. When ready to eat, prepare and preheat grill. Grill steak for 6–10 minutes, turning once, until desired doneness. Remove from grill and let stand, covered, for 10 minutes. Slice thinly against the grain and serve with the Chimichurri Sauce.

Nutrition Info:
- Info Per Serving: Calories:244.50; Fat:18.59 g ;Saturated fat: 5.20 g ;Sodium: 117.31 mg

Sirloin Meatballs In Sauce

Servings: 6
Cooking Time: X

Ingredients:
- 1 tablespoon olive oil
- 3 cloves garlic, minced
- ½ cup minced onion
- 2 egg whites
- ½ cup dry breadcrumbs
- ¼ cup grated Parmesan cheese
- ½ teaspoon crushed fennel seeds
- ½ teaspoon dried oregano leaves
- 2 teaspoons Worcestershire sauce
- 1/8 teaspoon pepper
- 1/8 teaspoon crushed red pepper flakes
- 1 pound 95% lean ground sirloin
- 1 recipe Spaghetti Sauce

Directions:
1. In small saucepan, heat olive oil over medium heat. Add garlic and onion; cook and stir until tender, about 5 minutes. Remove from heat and place in large mixing bowl.
2. Add egg whites, breadcrumbs, Parmesan, fennel, oregano, Worcestershire sauce, pepper, and pepper flakes and mix well. Add sirloin; mix gently but thoroughly until combined. Form into 12 meatballs.
3. In large nonstick saucepan, place Spaghetti Sauce and bring to a simmer. Carefully add meatballs to sauce. Return to a simmer, partially cover, and simmer for 15–25 minutes or until meatballs are thoroughly cooked.

Nutrition Info:
- Info Per Serving: Calories: 367.93; Fat: 13.56 g ;Saturated fat: 3.91 g;Sodium: 305.47 mg

Risotto With Ham And Pineapple

Servings: 4–6
Cooking Time: X

Ingredients:
- 2 cups water
- 2 cups Low-Fat Chicken Broth
- 1 tablespoon olive oil
- 1 tablespoon butter
- 1 onion, chopped
- 3 cloves garlic, minced
- ½ teaspoon dried thyme leaves
- 1 red bell pepper, chopped
- 1½ cups Arborio rice
- 1 cup chopped ham
- 1 (20-ounce) can pineapple tidbits, drained
- 1/8 teaspoon pepper
- ¼ cup grated Parmesan cheese

Directions:
1. In medium saucepan, combine water and chicken broth and bring to a simmer over low heat. Keep warm. In large saucepan, heat olive oil and butter over medium heat. Add onion and garlic; cook and stir for 3 minutes. Add thyme, bell pepper, and rice; cook and stir for 4 minutes.

2. Start adding the broth, 1 cup at a time, stirring frequently. When 1 cup broth remains to be added, add ham, pineapple, and pepper to risotto. Add last cup of broth; cook and stir until rice is tender and creamy and liquid is absorbed. Stir in Parmesan, cover, let stand for 5 minutes, then serve.

Nutrition Info:
- Info Per Serving: Calories:369.77; Fat: 8.92 g ;Saturated fat: 3.17 g ;Sodium: 390.26 mg

Mustard Pork Tenderloin

Servings: 6
Cooking Time: X

Ingredients:
- 2 tablespoons red wine
- 1 tablespoon sugar
- 1 tablespoon olive oil
- 1¼ pounds pork tenderloin
- ¼ cup low-fat sour cream
- 3 tablespoons Dijon mustard
- 1 tablespoon minced fresh chives

Directions:
1. In glass baking dish, combine red wine, sugar, and olive oil. Add pork tenderloin; turn to coat. Cover and refrigerate for 8 hours.
2. Preheat oven to 325ºF. Let pork stand at room temperature for 20 minutes. Roast for 30 minutes, basting occasionally with the marinade.
3. In small bowl, combine sour cream, mustard, and chives. Spread over the tenderloin. Continue roasting for 25–35 minutes or until pork registers 160ºF. Let stand for 5 minutes, then slice to serve.

Nutrition Info:
- Info Per Serving: Calories: 209.84 ; Fat:9.08 g ;Saturated fat: 2.98 g ;Sodium: 147.13 mg

Teriyaki Beef Skewers

Servings: 4
Cooking Time: 15 Minutes

Ingredients:
- ¾ pound top sirloin steak, cut into 1-inch cubes
- ¼ cup low-sodium beef broth
- 2 tablespoons rice wine vinegar
- 2 tablespoons fresh lemon juice
- 2 tablespoons honey
- 1 teaspoon toasted sesame oil
- 1 teaspoon hoisin sauce
- ¼ teaspoon garlic powder
- ¼ teaspoon ground ginger
- 2 yellow summer squash, cut into ½-inch slices
- 12 medium mushrooms, halved
- 2 red bell peppers, cut into ½-inch strips

Directions:
1. Prepare and preheat the grill to medium heat.
2. Trim any visible fat from the steak and discard, and cut the steak into 1-inch cubes. Put the steak in a medium bowl and add the beef broth, vinegar, lemon juice, honey, sesame oil, hoisin sauce, garlic powder, and ground ginger, and mix well.
3. Remove the steak from the broth mixture; reserve the mixture for basting. Thread the steak cubes onto skewers, alternating with the squash, mushrooms, and bell pepper.
4. Grill the skewers about 6 inches from the heat source for 3 minutes on one side; turn and brush with the broth mixture. Grill for 3 minutes on the second side. Turn and brush with the broth mixture on the other side.
5. Grill on the other two sides for 1 to 2 minutes each, brushing with the broth mixture right after the turn, until the beef registers 145°F for medium on a meat thermometer. Discard any remaining broth mixture, and serve immediately.

Nutrition Info:
- Info Per Serving: Calories: 279 ; Fat: 12 g ;Saturated fat: 4 g ;Sodium: 79 mg

Wasabi-roasted Filet Mignon

Servings: 12
Cooking Time: X

Ingredients:
- 1 (3-pound) filet mignon roast
- ¼ teaspoon pepper
- 1 teaspoon powdered wasabi
- 2 tablespoons sesame oil
- 2 tablespoons soy sauce

Directions:
1. Preheat oven to 400ºF. If the roast has a thin end and a thick end, fold the thin end under so the roast is about the same thickness. Place on roasting pan.
2. In small bowl, combine pepper, wasabi, oil, and soy sauce, and mix well. Brush half over roast. Roast the beef for 30 minutes, then remove and brush with remaining wasabi mixture. Return to oven for 5–10 minutes longer or until meat thermometer registers at

least 145ºF for medium rare.

3. Remove from oven, cover, and let stand for 15 minutes before slicing to serve.

Nutrition Info:
• Info Per Serving: Calories:298.15; Fat: 24.00g ;Saturated fat:8.99 g ;Sodium: 143.07 mg

Meatball Pizza

Servings: 6
Cooking Time: X

Ingredients:
• 1 Whole-Grain Pizza Crust , prebaked
• 1 tablespoon olive oil
• 1 onion, chopped
• 1 green bell pepper, chopped
• ½ cup shredded carrots
• 1 (6-ounce) can no-salt tomato paste
• 2 tablespoons mustard
• ¼ cup water
• 12 plain Sirloin Meatballs , baked
• 1 cup shredded extra-sharp Cheddar cheese
• ½ cup shredded part-skim mozzarella cheese

Directions:
1. Preheat oven to 400ºF. In medium saucepan, heat olive oil over medium heat. Add onion, bell pepper, and carrots; cook and stir until crisp-tender, about 5 minutes. Add tomato paste, mustard, and water and bring to a simmer. Simmer, stirring frequently, for 5 minutes.
2. Spread the sauce over the pizza crust. Cut the meatballs in half and arrange on the pizza. Sprinkle with Cheddar and mozzarella cheeses.
3. Bake for 20–30 minutes or until crust is golden brown, pizza is hot, and cheese is melted and bubbling. Let stand for 5 minutes, then serve.

Nutrition Info:
• Info Per Serving: Calories:437.80; Fat: 15.85 g ;Saturated fat: 6.29g ;Sodium: 432.76 mg

Chile Pork With Soba Noodles

Servings: 4
Cooking Time: 15 Minutes

Ingredients:
• 3 (4-ounce) boneless top loin pork chops
• Pinch salt
• 2 teaspoons chili powder
• ⅛ teaspoon cayenne pepper

• 1 cup low-sodium chicken broth
• 1 tablespoon rice wine vinegar
• 1 teaspoon low-sodium soy sauce
• 1 tablespoon cornstarch
• 8 ounces soba noodles
• 1 teaspoon toasted sesame oil
• 1 carrot, grated
• 1 red chile pepper, seeded and minced
• 2 scallions, chopped
• 1 small zucchini, sliced

Directions:
1. Bring a large pot of water to a boil.
2. Trim excess fat from the pork chops and discard. Cut the chops into 1-inch cubes, and put them in a medium bowl. Toss with the salt, chili powder, and cayenne pepper, and set aside.
3. In a small bowl, combine the chicken broth, rice wine vinegar, soy sauce, and cornstarch, and set aside.
4. Cook the soba noodles according to the package directions, about 6 minutes. Drain in a colander, rinse with cool water, and set aside.
5. In a large nonstick skillet or wok over medium-high heat, heat the sesame oil. Add the pork pieces and stir-fry 3 to 4 minutes or until the pork is almost cooked. Transfer to a clean plate.
6. Add the carrot, chile pepper, scallions, and zucchini to the skillet; stir-fry for 3 to 4 minutes or until crisp-tender.
7. Add the chicken broth mixture, the pork, and the soba noodles to the skillet, and stir-fry 2 to 3 minutes or until the sauce simmers and is thickened. Serve immediately.

Nutrition Info:
• Info Per Serving: Calories: 342 ; Fat: 5 g ;Saturated fat: 2 g ;Sodium: 542 mg

Canadian-bacon Risotto

Servings: 6
Cooking Time: X

Ingredients:
• 2 cups water
• 3 cups Low-Sodium Chicken Broth
• 1 tablespoon olive oil
• 1 chopped onion
• 3 cloves garlic, minced
• 1 (8-ounce) package sliced mushrooms
• ½ teaspoon dried oregano leaves
• 1 teaspoon dried basil leaves

- 2 cups Arborio rice
- 1/8 teaspoon white pepper
- 1 cup chopped Canadian bacon
- ¼ cup shredded Parmesan cheese
- 1 tablespoon butter

Directions:

1. In medium saucepan, combine water and broth; heat over low heat until warm; keep on heat.
2. In large saucepan, heat olive oil over medium heat. Add onion, garlic, and mushrooms to pan; cook and stir until crisp-tender, about 4 minutes. Add oregano and basil.
3. Add rice; cook and stir for 2 minutes. Add the broth mixture, a cup at a time, stirring until the liquid is absorbed, about 15 minutes. When there is 1 cup broth remaining, add pepper and Canadian bacon along with the last cup of broth. Cook and stir until rice is tender, about 5 minutes.
4. Stir in Parmesan and butter and serve immediately.

Nutrition Info:

- Info Per Serving: Calories: 379.72; Fat: 9.41 g ;Saturated fat:3.17g ;Sodium: 292.55 mg

Pan-seared Beef Tenderloin With Wild Mushrooms

Servings: X
Cooking Time: 25 Minutes

Ingredients:

- 2 (4-ounce) beef tenderloin steaks, fat trimmed
- Sea salt
- Freshly ground black pepper
- Nonstick olive oil cooking spray
- 1 tablespoon canola oil
- 1 teaspoon minced garlic
- 4 cups thinly sliced wild mushrooms (shiitake, oyster, portobello, and chanterelles)
- ½ teaspoon chopped fresh thyme

Directions:

1. Season the steaks lightly with salt and pepper.
2. Lightly coat a large skillet with cooking spray and place it over medium heat. Sear the steaks until they reach your desired doneness, 5 minutes per side for medium.
3. Remove the steaks and set aside.
4. Add the canola oil to the skillet and sauté the garlic until softened, about 3 minutes.
5. Add the mushrooms and cook, stirring occasionally,

until lightly caramelized, 7 to 8 minutes.
6. Stir in the thyme and season with salt and pepper.
7. Serve the steaks with the mushrooms.

Nutrition Info:

- Info Per Serving: Calories: 267 ; Fat: 15 g ;Saturated fat: 3 g ;Sodium: 72 mg

Beef Burrito Skillet

Servings: 4
Cooking Time: 15 Minutes

Ingredients:

- ¾ pound extra-lean ground beef
- 1 onion, chopped
- 4 cloves garlic, minced
- 1 jalapeño pepper, seeded and minced
- 1 tablespoon chili powder
- ½ teaspoon cumin
- 1 (16-ounce) can no-salt-added pinto beans, rinsed and drained
- 1 tomato, chopped
- 1 cup frozen corn, thawed
- ½ cup low-sodium salsa
- 3 corn tortillas, cut into 1-inch strips
- 2 tablespoons crumbled cotija cheese
- ¼ cup low-fat sour cream

Directions:

1. In a large skillet, sauté the ground beef, onion, garlic, and jalapeño pepper, stirring to break up the meat, until the beef is browned, about 5 to 7 minutes.
2. Add the chili powder and cumin, and stir.
3. Add in the pinto beans, tomato, corn, and salsa, and bring to a simmer. Simmer for 5 minutes, stirring occasionally.
4. Stir in the corn tortillas and cook for 3 to 4 minutes. Top with the cheese and sour cream, and serve.

Nutrition Info:

- Info Per Serving: Calories: 403 ; Fat: 10 g ;Saturated fat: 4 g ;Sodium: 215 mg

Pork Quesadillas

Servings: 6
Cooking Time: X

Ingredients:

- 1/3 cup low-fat sour cream
- 1 cup shredded part-skim mozzarella cheese
- 1 cup chopped Mustard Pork Tenderloin (below)
- 1 avocado, chopped

- 1 jalapeño pepper, minced
- 10 (6-inch) corn tortillas
- 2 tablespoons olive oil

Directions:

1. In medium bowl, combine sour cream, cheese, pork tenderloin, avocado, and jalapeño pepper and mix gently.
2. Divide mixture among half the tortillas, placing the remaining half of tortillas on top to make sandwiches. Heat griddle and brush with olive oil. Place quesadillas on the griddle; cover and grill for 2–3 minutes on each side until tortillas are crisp and cheese is melted. Cut into quarters and serve.

Nutrition Info:

- Info Per Serving: Calories: 315.36 ; Fat:16.67 g ;Saturated fat:5.55 g ;Sodium:161.17 mg

Sliced Flank Steak With Sherry-mustard Sauce

Servings: X
Cooking Time: 30 Minutes

Ingredients:

- 1 (6-ounce) flank steak, fat trimmed
- Sea salt
- Freshly ground black pepper
- Nonstick olive oil cooking spray
- 1 teaspoon canola oil
- 2 shallots, chopped
- ½ cup sherry
- 1 cup low-sodium beef broth
- 2 teaspoons Dijon mustard
- ½ teaspoon chopped fresh thyme

Directions:

1. Lightly season the steak with salt and pepper.
2. Generously coat a medium skillet with cooking spray and let it preheat over high heat on the stove. Sear the steak until browned and cooked to your desired doneness, 6 minutes per side for medium. Set the steak aside to rest.
3. While the steak is resting, warm the canola oil in the skillet. Add the shallots and sauté until softened, about 3 minutes.
4. Add the sherry to the skillet and bring to a boil. Cook until the liquid is reduced by half, about 4 minutes. Stir in the broth, mustard, and thyme and continue boiling until the sauce is reduced to about ½ cup, about 5 minutes.

5. Slice the steak thinly across the grain and serve with the sauce.

Nutrition Info:

- Info Per Serving: Calories: 268 ; Fat: 13 g ;Saturated fat: 5 g ;Sodium: 278 mg

Pork Chops With Smoky Barbecue Rub

Servings: X
Cooking Time: 15 Minutes

Ingredients:

- 2 (6-ounce) boneless pork top-loin chops
- 2 tablespoons Smoky Barbecue Rub
- 1 teaspoon chopped fresh cilantro, for garnish

Directions:

1. Preheat a grill to medium-high heat.
2. Season the pork all over with the rub.
3. Grill the pork until it is just cooked through, turning once, about 8 minutes per side.
4. Serve topped with cilantro.

Nutrition Info:

- Info Per Serving: Calories: 287 ; Fat: 17 g ;Saturated fat: 6 g ;Sodium: 513 mg

Filet Mignon With Capers

Servings: 2
Cooking Time: X

Ingredients:

- 2 (3-ounce) filet mignon steaks
- 1/8 teaspoon pepper
- 1 tablespoon grapeseed oil
- 2 cloves garlic, minced
- 2 tablespoons tiny capers, rinsed
- 1/3 cup dry red wine
- 2 teaspoons mustard

Directions:

1. Trim excess fat from the steaks and sprinkle with pepper. Heat grape-seed oil in medium saucepan over medium-high heat. Add steaks and cook until they can be moved and the bottom is browned, about 4–5 minutes. Carefully turn steaks and add garlic to the pan.
2. Cook steaks 4 minutes longer for medium rare, 5 minutes longer for medium, and 6 minutes longer for medium-well done. Remove steaks from pan and cover with foil to keep warm.
3. Drain capers and add to drippings in skillet along with wine. Bring to a boil, scraping pan to loosen drip-

pings. Boil for 1 minute to reduce slightly. Then turn off the heat, whisk in the mustard, and serve sauce with steaks.

Nutrition Info:
- Info Per Serving: Calories: 244.62 ; Fat: 12.13g ;Saturated fat:4.01 g ;Sodium: 360.50 mg

Prosciutto Fruit Omelet

Servings: 4
Cooking Time: X

Ingredients:
- ¼ pound thinly sliced prosciutto
- ½ cup shredded part-skim mozzarella cheese
- 2 tablespoons grated Parmesan cheese
- 1 egg
- 8 egg whites
- ¼ cup low-fat sour cream
- 1/8 teaspoon pepper
- 1 tablespoon olive oil
- 1 apple, chopped

Directions:
1. Trim off excess fat from prosciutto and discard. Thinly slice the pro-sciutto and combine with the mozzarella and Parmesan cheeses. Set aside.
2. In large bowl, combine egg, egg whites, sour cream, and pepper and mix well. In large nonstick saucepan, heat olive oil over medium heat; add apples and stir until apples are tender. Pour in egg mixture.
3. Cook, running spatula around edges to let uncooked mixture flow underneath, until eggs are almost set and bottom is golden brown.
4. Sprinkle with cheese and ham mixture and cook for 2–3 minutes longer. Cover, remove from heat, and let stand for 2 minutes. Fold omelet over on itself and slide onto plate to serve.

Nutrition Info:
- Info Per Serving: Calories:221.48; Fat:12.35 g ;Saturated fat:4.99 g ;Sodium: 551.41 mg

Skillet Beef Macaroni

Servings: X
Cooking Time: 20 Minutes

Ingredients:
- 2 teaspoons olive oil
- 6 ounces extra-lean ground beef
- 2 celery stalks, chopped
- ½ cup chopped sweet onion
- 1 teaspoon minced garlic
- 1 cup Double Tomato Sauce or your favorite low-sodium marinara sauce
- 1 tablespoon tomato paste
- 1 teaspoon chopped fresh oregano
- 1 teaspoon chopped fresh basil
- Pinch red pepper flakes
- 2 cups cooked whole-grain elbow pasta

Directions:
1. In a large skillet, warm the oil over medium-high heat.
2. Add the ground beef and cook until browned, about 6 minutes.
3. Add the celery, onions, and garlic and sauté until softened, about 4 minutes.
4. Stir in the tomato sauce, tomato paste, oregano, basil, and red pepper flakes and bring the sauce to a boil.
5. Reduce the heat to low and simmer the sauce for 10 minutes to allow the flavors to meld.
6. Stir in the pasta and serve.

Nutrition Info:
- Info Per Serving: Calories: 377; Fat: 10 g ;Saturated fat: 2 g ;Sodium: 312 mg

Simple Pork Burgers

Servings: X
Cooking Time: 15 Minutes

Ingredients:
- ½ pound extra-lean ground pork
- 1 large egg white
- 1 scallion, white parts only, chopped
- ¼ cup ground almonds
- ¼ teaspoon minced garlic
- ⅛ teaspoon allspice
- Sea salt
- Freshly ground black pepper

Directions:
1. Preheat a grill to medium-high heat.
2. In a medium bowl, thoroughly mix together the pork, egg white, scallion, almonds, garlic, and allspice. Season the mixture with salt and pepper.
3. Form the mixture into 2 burgers.
4. Place the burgers on the grill and cook until they are just cooked through, 7 to 8 minutes per side, depending on the thickness of the patties.
5. Serve with your favorite toppings.

Nutrition Info:
- Info Per Serving: Calories: 243 ; Fat: 13 g ;Saturated fat: 3 g ;Sodium: 83 mg

Pork Chops With Cabbage

Servings: 6
Cooking Time: X

Ingredients:
- 1 red onion, chopped
- 4 cloves garlic, minced
- 3 cups chopped red cabbage
- 3 cups chopped green cabbage
- 1 apple, chopped
- 6 (3-ounce) boneless pork chops
- 1/8 teaspoon white pepper
- 1 tablespoon olive oil
- ¼ cup brown sugar
- ¼ cup apple cider vinegar
- 1 tablespoon mustard

Directions:

1. In 4- to 5-quart slow cooker, combine onion, garlic, cabbages, and apple and mix well.

2. Trim pork chops of any excess fat and sprinkle with pepper. Heat olive oil in large saucepan over medium heat. Brown chops on just one side, about 3 minutes. Add to slow cooker with vegetables.

3. In small bowl, combine brown sugar, vinegar, and mustard and mix well. Pour into slow cooker. Cover and cook on low for 7–8 hours or until pork and cabbage are tender. Serve immediately.

Nutrition Info:
- Info Per Serving: Calories: 242.86 ; Fat: 10.57 g ;Saturated fat:3.37 g ;Sodium:364.80 mg

Corned-beef Hash

Servings: 6
Cooking Time: X

Ingredients:
- 2 tablespoons olive oil
- 2 onions, chopped
- 4 cloves garlic, minced
- 8 fingerling potatoes, chopped
- 4 carrots, chopped
- ¼ cup water
- ½ pound deli corned beef, diced
- 1/8 teaspoon ground cloves
- 1/8 teaspoon white pepper
- 3 tablespoons low-sodium chili sauce

Directions:

1. Place olive oil in large saucepan; heat over medium heat. Add onion and garlic; cook and stir for 3 minutes. Add potatoes and carrots; cook and stir until potatoes are partially cooked, about 5 minutes.

2. Add water, corned beef, cloves, pepper, and chili sauce. Stir well, then cover, reduce heat to low, and simmer for 10–15 minutes or until blended and potatoes are cooked. Serve immediately.

Nutrition Info:
- Info Per Serving: Calories: 283.21 ; Fat:11.97 g ;Saturated fat: 3.09 g;Sodium:472.63 mg

VEGETARIAN MAINS

Vegetarian Mains

Wild Rice & Lentils

Servings: 6
Cooking Time: 40 Min

Ingredients:
- 5 cups water
- 1 tsp sea salt, divided
- 1 cup wild rice
- 1 cup dried brown lentils, picked over
- ¼ cup olive oil
- 2 large brown onions, thinly sliced
- ½ cup cilantro, finely chopped
- 6 spring onions, thinly sliced, divided
- Ground black pepper

Directions:
1. In a large stockpot, add the water and add ¾ tsp salt, boil over high heat.
2. Add the rice and cook for 10 minutes, then lower the heat to a simmer.
3. Add the lentils and simmer. Cover the stockpot and reduce the heat to medium-low. Cook for 20 to 25 minutes, or until the rice and lentils are fully cooked. Remove from the heat.
4. Drain any remaining liquid and rest for 10 minutes.
5. In a large, heavy-bottom pan, heat the olive oil over medium heat. Line a plate with paper towels.
6. Once the oil is hot, add the onions and cook for 20 to 25 minutes, or until nicely browned, stirring frequently. Use a slotted spoon to transfer the onions onto the lined plate. Sprinkle with the remaining ¼ tsp salt.
7. Mix half of the onions, cilantro, and half the spring onion into the lentil and rice mixture.
8. Serve the lentil and rice in bowls and garnish with the remaining onions, spring onion, and pepper. Serve warm.

Nutrition Info:
- Info Per Serving: Calories: 333 ; Fat: 10 g ;Saturated fat: 7 g ;Sodium: 399 mg

Farro Sloppy Joes

Servings: X
Cooking Time: 20 Minutes

Ingredients:
- ¾ cup uncooked pearled farro, rinsed well
- 1 cup water
- 1 teaspoon olive oil
- 1 red bell pepper, chopped
- ½ cup sweet onion, finely chopped
- 1 teaspoon minced garlic
- 1 (15-ounce) can low-sodium diced tomatoes, with their juices
- 1 teaspoon maple syrup
- 1 teaspoon low-sodium tamari sauce
- ½ teaspoon chili powder
- ¼ teaspoon dry mustard
- ¼ teaspoon dried oregano
- 2 whole-grain hamburger rolls, for serving

Directions:
1. In a small saucepan, combine the farro with the water. Bring to a boil over high heat and then reduce the heat to low. Cover and simmer until the water is absorbed, 15 to 20 minutes. Drain any excess water.
2. While the farro is cooking, warm the oil in a medium skillet and sauté the bell pepper, onions, and garlic until softened, about 3 minutes.
3. Stir in the tomatoes, maple syrup, tamari, chili powder, mustard, and oregano and bring the sauce to a boil. Reduce the heat to low and simmer for 5 to 7 minutes, stirring occasionally.
4. Remove the sauce from the heat and stir in the cooked farro.
5. Divide the sloppy joe mixture between the rolls and serve.

Nutrition Info:
- Info Per Serving: Calories: 407 ; Fat: 6 g ;Saturated fat: 1 g ;Sodium: 282 mg

Cheese-and-veggie Stuffed Artichokes

Servings: 4
Cooking Time: X

Ingredients:
- 1 cup shredded Havarti cheese
- 2 tablespoons grated Parmesan cheese
- ¼ cup plain yogurt
- ¼ cup low-fat mayonnaise
- 1 tablespoon lemon juice
- 2 scallions, chopped
- 1 tablespoon capers
- 1 cup grated carrots
- 1 cup grape tomatoes
- 1/8 teaspoon salt
- 4 globe artichokes
- 1 lemon, cut into wedges

Directions:
1. In medium bowl, combine Havarti, Parmesan, yogurt, mayonnaise, lemon juice, scallions, and capers and mix well. Stir in carrots, tomatoes, and salt, and set aside.
2. Cut off the top inch of the artichokes. Cut off the sharp tip of each leaf. Pull off the tough outer leaves and discard. Rub cut edges with lemon wedges. Cut artichokes in half lengthwise.
3. Bring a large pot of salted water to a boil and add lemon wedges. Add artichokes and simmer for 20–25 minutes or until a leaf pulls out easily from the artichoke. Cool, then carefully remove choke with spoon.
4. Stuff artichokes with the cheese mixture, place on serving plate, cover, and chill for 2–4 hours before serving.

Nutrition Info:
- Info Per Serving: Calories: 266.61; Fat:14.24 g ;Saturated fat:6.47 g ;Sodium: 413.37 mg

Corn-and-chili Pancakes

Servings: 6
Cooking Time: X

Ingredients:
- ½ cup buttermilk
- 1 tablespoon olive oil
- ½ cup egg substitute
- ½ cup grated extra-sharp Cheddar cheese
- 1 jalapeño pepper, minced
- 2 ears sweet corn
- ½ cup cornmeal
- 1 cup all-purpose flour
- 1½ teaspoons baking powder
- ½ teaspoon baking soda
- 1 tablespoon sugar
- 1 tablespoon chili powder
- 1 tablespoon peanut oil
- 1 tablespoon butter

Directions:
1. In large bowl, combine buttermilk, olive oil, egg substitute, Cheddar, and jalapeño pepper and mix well.
2. Cut the kernels off the sweet corn and add to buttermilk mixture along with cornmeal, flour, baking powder, baking soda, sugar, and chili powder; mix until combined. Let stand for 10 minutes.
3. Heat griddle or frying pan over medium heat. Brush with the butter, then add the batter, ¼ cup at a time. Cook until bubbles form and start to break and sides look dry, about 3–4 minutes. Carefully flip pancakes and cook until light golden brown on second side, about 2–3 minutes. Serve immediately.

Nutrition Info:
- Info Per Serving: Calories:252.62; Fat: 9.20 g ;Saturated fat:3.03 g ;Sodium:287.01 mg

Spinach-ricotta Omelet

Servings: 4
Cooking Time: X

Ingredients:
- 1 (10-ounce) package frozen chopped spinach, thawed and drained
- ½ cup part-skim ricotta cheese
- 2 tablespoons grated Parmesan cheese
- 1/8 teaspoon nutmeg
- 7 egg whites
- 1 egg yolk
- ¼ cup milk
- 1/8 teaspoon pepper
- 1 tablespoon olive oil
- ¼ cup finely chopped onion

Directions:
1. Press spinach between layers of paper towel to remove all excess moisture. Set aside. In small bowl, combine ricotta with Parmesan cheese and nutmeg; set aside.
2. In medium bowl, beat egg whites until a soft foam forms. In small bowl, combine egg yolk with milk and pepper and beat well.

3. Heat a nonstick skillet over medium heat. Add olive oil, then add spinach and onion; cook and stir until onion is crisp-tender, about 4 minutes. Meanwhile, fold egg-yolk mixture into beaten egg whites. Add egg mixture to skillet; cook, running spatula around edges to let uncooked mixture flow underneath, until eggs are set but still moist.

4. Spoon ricotta mixture on top of eggs; cover pan, and let cook for 2 minutes. Then fold omelet and serve immediately.

Nutrition Info:
• Info Per Serving: Calories: 162.81; Fat:8.74 g ;Saturated fat: 3.23 g ;Sodium: 245.82 mg

Tofu And Root Vegetable Curry

Servings: X
Cooking Time: 25 Minutes

Ingredients:
• 2 teaspoons olive oil
• 1 cup small cauliflower florets
• 1 parsnip, diced
• 1 carrot, diced
• 1 red bell pepper, thinly sliced
• 1 cup diced sweet potato
• 1 teaspoon peeled, grated fresh ginger
• ½ teaspoon minced garlic
• 1 cup low-sodium vegetable broth
• 2 tomatoes, chopped
• 2 cups diced extra-firm tofu
• 2 tablespoons curry powder or paste
• ¼ cup chopped cashews, for garnish

Directions:
1. In a large saucepan, warm the olive oil over medium-high heat.
2. Add the cauliflower, parsnips, carrots, bell peppers, sweet potatoes, ginger, and garlic and sauté until the vegetables begin to soften, about 10 minutes.
3. Stir in the vegetable broth, tomatoes, tofu, and curry powder and bring the mixture to a boil.
4. Reduce the heat to low and simmer until the vegetables are tender and everything is completely heated through, 15 to 18 minutes.
5. Serve topped with cashews.

Nutrition Info:
• Info Per Serving: Calories: 457 ; Fat: 20 g ;Saturated fat: 3 g ;Sodium: 135 mg

Pinto Bean Tortillas

Servings: 4
Cooking Time: 25 Min

Ingredients:
• 1 (15 oz) can low-sodium pinto beans, rinsed and drained
• ¼ cup canned fire-roasted tomato salsa
• ¾ cup dairy-free cheddar cheese, shredded and divided
• 1 medium red bell pepper, seeded, chopped and divided
• 2 tbsp. olive oil, divided
• 4 large, wholegrain tortillas

Directions:
1. Place the drained pinto beans and the tomato salsa together in a food processor. Process until smooth.
2. Spread ½ cup of the pinto bean mixture on each tortilla. Sprinkle each tortilla with 3 tbsp. of dairy-free cheddar cheese and ¼ cup of red bell pepper. Fold in half and repeat with the remaining tortillas.
3. Add 1 tbsp. of olive oil to a large, heavy-bottom pan over medium heat until hot. Place the first two folded tortillas in the pan. Cover and cook for 2 minutes until the tortillas are crispy on the bottom. Flip and cook for 2 minutes until crispy on the other side.
4. Repeat with the remaining folded tortillas and the remaining olive oil. Keep warm until ready to serve.

Nutrition Info:
• Info Per Serving: Calories:438 ; Fat: 21 g ;Saturated fat: 5 g ;Sodium: 561 mg

Crisp Polenta With Tomato Sauce

Servings: 8
Cooking Time: X

Ingredients:
• 1 recipe Cheese Polenta
• 1 cup shredded part-skim mozzarella cheese
• 3 cups Spaghetti Sauce , heated

Directions:
1. Prepare polenta as directed, except when done, pour onto a greased cookie sheet; spread to a ½"-thick rectangle, about 9" × 15". Cover and chill until very firm, about 2 hours.
2. Preheat broiler. Cut polenta into fifteen 3" squares. Place on broiler pan; broil for 4–6 minutes or until golden brown. Carefully turn polenta and broil for 3–5 minutes or until golden brown.

3. Remove from oven and sprinkle with mozzarella cheese. Top each with a dollop of the hot Spaghetti Sauce, and serve immediately.

Nutrition Info:
• Info Per Serving: Calories: 229.70 ; Fat:8.43 g ;Saturated fat: 4.20 g ;Sodium: 260.08 mg

Ratatouille

Servings: 6
Cooking Time: X

Ingredients:
• 3 tablespoons olive oil
• 2 onions, chopped
• 4 cloves garlic, minced
• 1 green bell pepper, sliced
• 1 yellow bell pepper, sliced
• 1 eggplant, peeled and cubed
• ¼ teaspoon salt
• 1/8 teaspoon pepper
• 2 tablespoons flour
• 2 zucchini, sliced
• 1 tablespoon red-wine vinegar
• 2 tablespoons capers, rinsed
• ¼ cup chopped flat-leaf parsley

Directions:
1. In large saucepan, heat olive oil over medium heat. Add onion and garlic; cook and stir until crisp-tender, about 3 minutes. Add bell peppers; cook and stir until crisp-tender, about 3 minutes.
2. Sprinkle eggplant with salt, pepper, and flour. Add to saucepan; cook and stir until eggplant begins to soften. Add remaining ingredients except parsley; cover, and simmer for 30–35 minutes or until vegetables are soft and mixture is blended. Sprinkle with parsley and serve.

Nutrition Info:
• Info Per Serving: Calories:124.26; Fat:7.10 g ;Saturated fat:1.02 g ;Sodium: 187.22 mg

Curried Garbanzo Beans

Servings: 4
Cooking Time: 15 Min

Ingredients:
• 2 tbsp. coconut oil
• 1 tbsp. garlic, crushed
• 1 (15 oz) can low-sodium garbanzo beans, drained and rinsed

• 1 (15 oz) can low-sodium diced tomatoes with their juices
• 1 tsp mild or hot curry powder
• ½ tsp fine sea salt
• ¼ tsp ground black pepper
• 4 cups baby spinach

Directions:
1. In a large, heavy-bottom pan, heat the coconut oil over medium heat.
2. Add the garlic and cook for 20 seconds, until fragrant.
3. Add the garbanzo beans, tomatoes with their juices, mild or hot curry powder, fine sea salt and pepper, mix to combine. Simmer for 10 minutes, stirring regularly, or until the flavours come together.
4. Add the baby spinach and stir for 1 to 2 minutes, until the spinach has wilted. Remove from the heat and serve immediately.

Nutrition Info:
• Info Per Serving: Calories: 168 ; Fat: 9 g ;Saturated fat: 1 g ;Sodium: 352 mg

Chickpeas In Lettuce Wraps

Servings: 6–8
Cooking Time: X

Ingredients:
• 1 (15-ounce) can no-salt chickpeas
• 3 tablespoons olive oil
• 3 tablespoons lemon juice
• 3 cloves garlic, minced
• 1 tablespoon chopped fresh mint
• ½ cup diced red onion
• 8 lettuce leaves
• 1 cup chopped tomatoes
• 1 cup chopped yellow bell pepper

Directions:
1. Drain the chickpeas; rinse, and drain again. Place half in a blender or food processor. Add olive oil, lemon juice, garlic, and mint. Blend or process until smooth.
2. Place in medium bowl and stir in remaining chickpeas and red onion; stir until combined.
3. To make sandwiches, place lettuce leaves on work surface. Divide chickpea mixture among leaves and top with tomatoes and bell pepper. Roll up, folding in sides, to enclose filling. Serve immediately.

Nutrition Info:

- Info Per Serving: Calories:148.96; Fat:6.56 g ;Saturated fat:0.87 g ;Sodium: 6.80 g

Baba Ghanoush With Fennel Stew

Servings: X
Cooking Time: 42 Minutes

Ingredients:
- 2 small eggplants, cut in half and scored with a crosshatch pattern on the cut sides
- 2 teaspoons olive oil
- 1 cup chopped fennel
- ½ cup chopped sweet onion
- 1 teaspoon minced garlic
- ½ teaspoon ground cumin
- ¼ teaspoon ground coriander
- 4 cups low-sodium vegetable broth
- 2 tablespoons tahini
- Juice of ½ lemon
- 2 tomatoes, chopped
- Sea salt
- Freshly ground black pepper
- 1 teaspoon chopped fresh parsley, for garnish

Directions:
1. Preheat the oven to 400°F.
2. Line a baking sheet with parchment paper and place the eggplant, cut-side down, on the sheet.
3. Roast the eggplant until soft and collapsed, 20 to 25 minutes. Remove from the oven and set aside to cool slightly for 10 minutes.
4. In a large saucepan, warm the olive oil over medium-high heat. Add the fennel, onion, garlic, cumin, and coriander and sauté until softened, 6 to 7 minutes.
5. Discarding the skin, place the roasted eggplant into a blender or food processor. Add the vegetable broth, tahini, and lemon juice and purée until smooth.
6. Add the puréed eggplant to the saucepan and stir in the tomatoes. Bring the mixture to a boil, then reduce the heat to low and simmer 10 minutes.
7. Season with salt and pepper.
8. Serve topped with parsley.

Nutrition Info:
- Info Per Serving: Calories: 338 ; Fat: 14 g ;Saturated fat: 2 g ;Sodium: 287 mg

Chili-sautéed Tofu With Almonds

Servings: X
Cooking Time: 15 Minutes

Ingredients:
- 2 teaspoons olive oil
- ½ jalapeño pepper, chopped
- 1 teaspoon grated fresh ginger
- 1 teaspoon minced garlic
- 12 ounces extra-firm tofu, drained and cut into
- 1-inch cubes
- 2 cups shredded bok choy
- 1 red bell pepper, thinly sliced
- 1 scallion, white and green parts, thinly sliced
- 1 tablespoon low-sodium tamari sauce
- 1 tablespoon freshly squeezed lime juice
- 1 cup cooked quinoa, for serving
- ¼ cup chopped almonds, for garnish

Directions:
1. In a large skillet, warm the olive oil over medium-high heat.
2. Add the jalapeño, ginger, and garlic and sauté until softened, about 4 minutes.
3. Add the tofu, bok choy, bell peppers, and scallions and sauté until the tofu is lightly browned and the vegetables are tender, 8 to 10 minutes.
4. Stir in the tamari sauce and lime juice and toss to coat the ingredients.
5. Serve over quinoa, topped with chopped almonds.

Nutrition Info:
- Info Per Serving: Calories: 469 ; Fat: 24 g ;Saturated fat: 2 g ;Sodium: 279 mg

Sesame Soba Noodles

Servings: X
Cooking Time: 10 Minutes

Ingredients:
- 1 (4-ounce) package uncooked soba noodles
- 2 teaspoons sesame oil
- 1 teaspoon minced garlic
- 2 cups broccoli florets
- 1 cup snow peas, stringed
- 1 red bell pepper, thinly sliced
- 1 carrot, thinly sliced
- 1 cup bean sprouts
- ½ teaspoon low-sodium tamari sauce
- ½ scallion, white and green parts, thinly sliced
- 1 tablespoon sesame seeds, for garnish

Directions:

1. Cook the noodles according to the package directions with no added salt or oil. Drain and set aside in a large bowl.
2. In a large skillet, warm the sesame oil over medium-high heat. Add the garlic and sauté for 3 minutes.
3. Add the broccoli, snow peas, bell peppers, and carrots to the skillet and sauté until the vegetables are tender-crisp, 6 to 7 minutes.
4. Add the bean sprouts, tamari, and scallions and sauté for 1 more minute.
5. Add the soba noodles to the skillet and toss to combine.
6. Serve topped with sesame seeds.

Nutrition Info:

• Info Per Serving: Calories: 384 ; Fat: 8 g ;Saturated fat: 1 g ;Sodium: 358 mg

Pumpkin And Chickpea Patties

Servings: X
Cooking Time: 20 Minutes

Ingredients:

• 2 teaspoons olive oil, divided
• 2 cups grated fresh pumpkin
• ½ cup grated carrot
• ½ teaspoon minced garlic
• 2 cups low-sodium chickpeas, rinsed and drained
• ½ cup ground almonds
• 2 large egg whites
• 1 scallion, white and green parts, chopped
• ½ teaspoon chopped fresh thyme
• Sea salt
• Freshly ground black pepper

Directions:

1. Preheat the oven to 400°F.
2. Line a baking sheet with parchment paper and set aside.
3. In a large skillet, heat ½ teaspoon olive oil over medium-high heat. Add the pumpkin, carrots, and garlic and sauté until softened, about 4 minutes. Remove from the heat and transfer to a food processor. Wipe the skillet clean with paper towels.
4. Add the chickpeas, almonds, egg whites, scallions, and thyme to the food processor. Pulse until the mixture holds together when pressed.
5. Season with salt and pepper and divide the pumpkin mixture into 8 equal patties, flattening them to about ½-inch thick.

6. Heat the remaining 1½ teaspoons olive oil in the skillet. Cook the patties until lightly browned, about 4 minutes on each side.
7. Place the skillet in the oven and bake for an additional 5 minutes, until the patties are completely heated through.
8. Serve.

Nutrition Info:

• Info Per Serving: Calories: 560 ; Fat: 25 g ;Saturated fat: 3 g ;Sodium: 62 mg

Kidney Bean Stew

Servings: 4
Cooking Time: 25 Min

Ingredients:

• 2 tsp avocado oil
• 1 leek, thinly sliced
• ½ brown onion, finely chopped
• 1 tsp garlic, minced
• 3 cups low-sodium vegetable stock
• 1 cup Roma tomatoes, chopped
• 2 medium carrots, peeled and thinly sliced
• 1 cup cauliflower florets
• 1 cup broccoli florets
• 1 green bell pepper, seeds removed and diced
• 1 cup low-sodium canned kidney beans, rinsed and drained
• Pinch red pepper flakes
• Himalayan pink salt
• Ground black pepper
• 2 tbsp. low-fat Parmesan cheese, grated for garnish
• 1 tbsp. parsley, chopped for garnish

Directions:

1. In a large-sized stockpot, warm the avocado oil over medium-high heat.
2. Add the sliced leek, chopped onions, and minced garlic and fry for 4 minutes until softened.
3. Add the vegetable stock, tomatoes, carrots, cauliflower, broccoli, green bell peppers, kidney beans, and red pepper flakes, mix to combine.
4. Bring the stew to a boil, then reduce the heat to low and simmer for 18 to 20 minutes until the vegetables are tender.
5. Season with salt and pepper to taste.
6. Top with Parmesan cheese and parsley.

Nutrition Info:

• Info Per Serving: Calories:270 ; Fat: 8g ;Saturated fat: 3g ;Sodium: 237 mg

Homestyle Bean Soup

Servings: 6
Cooking Time: 20 Min

Ingredients:
- 6 cups low-sodium vegetable stock
- 2 (15 oz) cans low-sodium kidney beans, drained and rinsed
- 1 (16 oz) can pinto beans, drained and rinsed
- 1 (15 oz) can diced tomatoes with their juices
- ½ tsp Italian seasoning
- 1 cup carrots, finely chopped
- 1 cup celery stalk, finely chopped
- Himalayan pink salt
- Ground black pepper

Directions:
1. In a large-sized stockpot, add the vegetable stock, kidney beans, pinto beans, tomatoes in their juice, Italian seasoning, carrots, and celery, mix to combine.
2. Bring to a simmer over medium heat. Cook for 15 minutes, or until heated through. Remove from the heat and season with salt and pepper to taste. Serve hot.

Nutrition Info:
- Info Per Serving: Calories: 238 ; Fat: 1 g ;Saturated fat: 0 g ;Sodium: 135 mg

Savory French Toast

Servings: 4–6
Cooking Time: X

Ingredients:
- 1 tablespoon olive oil
- 1 tablespoon butter
- 1 onion, chopped
- 4 (1-inch thick) slices Light Whole-Grain Bread
- 1 cup shredded Jarlsberg cheese
- 1 egg
- 1 egg white
- 1/3 cup buttermilk
- 1 teaspoon dried thyme leaves
- ½ teaspoon hot sauce
- 1 cup Spaghetti Sauce

Directions:
1. In large saucepan, combine olive oil and butter over medium heat. Add onion; cook and stir until tender, about 5 minutes. Continue cooking until onion begins to turn golden, about 5–8 minutes longer. Remove onion from pan and place in small bowl. Remove pan from heat.
2. Let onion cool for 15 minutes. Meanwhile, cut a pocket in the center of each slice of bread. Add Jarlsberg to the onion mixture and mix. Stuff this into the bread pockets.
3. In shallow bowl, combine egg, egg whites, buttermilk, thyme, and hot sauce, and beat well. Dip stuffed bread into egg mixture, turning to coat.
4. Return saucepan to heat. Sauté the stuffed bread, turning once, about 4–5 minutes on each side until golden brown. Serve with the warmed Spaghetti Sauce.

Nutrition Info:
- Info Per Serving: Calories: 342.51 ; Fat: 14.56 g ;Saturated fat: 6.14 g ;Sodium: 198.74 mg

Quinoa-stuffed Peppers

Servings: 6
Cooking Time: X

Ingredients:
- 1 recipe Quinoa Pepper Pilaf
- ½ cup chopped flat-leaf parsley
- 1 cup shredded Havarti cheese
- 6 large red bell peppers
- 2 cups Spaghetti Sauce

Directions:
1. Preheat oven to 350ºF. Prepare pilaf and fluff. Stir in parsley and Havarti. Cut tops from peppers and remove seeds and membranes.
2. Spray 9" × 13" baking dish with nonstick cooking spray. Place a layer of Spaghetti Sauce in the dish. Stuff peppers with pilaf and arrange on sauce. Pour remaining sauce over and around peppers.
3. Bake for 50–60 minutes or until peppers are tender. Serve immediately.

Nutrition Info:
- Info Per Serving: Calories: 406.04 ; Fat:15.40 g ;Saturated fat: 4.69 g ;Sodium: 468.06 mg

Potato Soufflé

Servings: 4
Cooking Time: X

Ingredients:

- 2 Yukon Gold potatoes
- 1 tablespoon olive oil
- 1/8 teaspoon nutmeg
- ¼ teaspoon onion salt
- 1/8 teaspoon cayenne pepper
- 1/3 cup fat-free half-and-half
- ¼ cup grated Parmesan cheese
- 4 egg whites
- ¼ teaspoon cream of tartar
- 1 cup chopped grape tomatoes
- ¼ cup chopped fresh basil

Directions:

1. Preheat oven to 450ºF. Peel and thinly slice potatoes, adding to a pot of cold water as you work. Bring potatoes to a boil over high heat, reduce heat, and simmer until tender, about 12–15 minutes.
2. Drain potatoes and return to hot pot; shake for 1 minute. Add olive oil, nutmeg, salt, and pepper and mash until smooth. Beat in the half-and-half and Parmesan.
3. In large bowl, combine egg whites with cream of tartar and beat until stiff peaks form. Stir a dollop of the egg whites into the potato mixture and stir. Then fold in remaining egg whites.
4. Spray the bottom of a 2-quart casserole with non-stick cooking spray. Spoon potato mixture into casserole. Bake for 20 minutes, then reduce heat to 375ºF and bake for another 12–17 minutes or until soufflé is golden brown and puffed.
5. While soufflé is baking, combine tomatoes and basil in small bowl and mix gently. Serve immediately with tomato mixture for topping the soufflé.

Nutrition Info:

- Info Per Serving: Calories: 224.39; Fat:9.11 g ;Saturated fat:2.24 g ;Sodium: 260.97 mg

Cannellini Bean–stuffed Sweet Potatoes

Servings: X
Cooking Time: 25 Minutes

Ingredients:

- 2 large sweet potatoes
- 1 teaspoon olive oil
- 1 cup low-sodium canned white cannellini beans, rinsed and drained
- 1 red bell pepper, chopped
- ½ cup chopped sweet onion
- 1 teaspoon minced garlic
- 1 cup shredded kale
- 1 tomato, chopped
- 1 teaspoon chopped fresh basil
- ½ teaspoon chopped fresh oregano
- Sea salt
- Freshly ground black pepper
- 2 tablespoons roasted pumpkin seeds, for garnish

Directions:

1. Preheat the oven to 350°F.
2. Pierce the sweet potatoes with a fork and place them in an 8-by-8-inch baking dish. Bake until tender, about 45 minutes.
3. While the potatoes are baking, warm the olive oil in a medium skillet over medium-high heat. Add the cannellini beans, bell peppers, onions, and garlic and sauté until heated through and tender, about 10 minutes.
4. Stir in the kale, tomatoes, basil, and oregano and sauté until the greens are wilted, about 3 minutes.
5. Season the bean mixture with salt and pepper.
6. Cut each baked potato in half lengthwise from end to end. Scoop out about half of the sweet potato flesh, reserving it for use in another meal or recipe. Spoon the bean mixture into the potatoes.
7. Serve topped with pumpkin seeds.

Nutrition Info:

- Info Per Serving: Calories: 406 ; Fat: 11 g ;Saturated fat: 2 g ;Sodium: 96 mg

Spaghetti Squash Skillet

Servings: X
Cooking Time: 35 Minutes

Ingredients:
- 1 (2-pound) spaghetti squash
- 1 tablespoon olive oil, divided
- Sea salt
- Freshly ground black pepper
- ½ cup chopped sweet onion
- 1 teaspoon minced garlic
- 1 orange bell pepper, diced
- 16 asparagus spears, woody ends trimmed, cut into 2-inch pieces
- ½ cup sliced sun-dried tomatoes
- 2 cups shredded kale
- 1 tablespoon chopped fresh basil

Directions:
1. Preheat the oven to 400°F.
2. Line a baking sheet with parchment paper and set aside.
3. Slice the squash in half lengthwise and scoop out the seeds. Place the squash, cut-side up, on the baking sheet. Brush the cut edges and hollows with 1 teaspoon olive oil and season lightly with salt and pepper.
4. Roast the squash until a knife can be inserted easily into the thickest section, 30 to 35 minutes.
5. Remove from the oven and let the squash cool for 10 minutes, then use a fork to shred the flesh into a medium bowl. Set aside.
6. While the squash is cooling, warm the remaining 2 teaspoons olive oil in a medium skillet over medium heat. Add the onions and garlic and sauté until softened, about 3 minutes.
7. Stir in the bell pepper, asparagus, sun-dried tomatoes, and kale and sauté until the vegetables and greens are tender, about 5 minutes.
8. Add the shredded spaghetti squash and basil and toss to combine.
9. Serve.

Nutrition Info:
- Info Per Serving: Calories: 340 ; Fat:10 g ;Saturated fat: 2 g ;Sodium: 287 mg

Sour-cream-and-herb Omelet

Servings: 4
Cooking Time: X

Ingredients:
- 1 tablespoon olive oil
- 2 shallots, minced
- 1 clove garlic, minced
- 2 cups egg substitute
- ¼ cup skim milk
- ¼ cup low-fat sour cream 1 teaspoon grated lemon zest
- 1 teaspoon fresh thyme leaves
- 1/8 teaspoon pepper
- 2/3 cup shredded extra-sharp Cheddar cheese

Directions:
1. In a large nonstick skillet, heat olive oil over medium heat. Add shallots and garlic; stir-fry for 2 minutes, until fragrant.
2. In medium bowl, combine egg substitute and milk and beat well. Add to saucepan; cook, running a spatula around the edges, and lifting the edges to let uncooked mixture flow underneath. Cook until eggs are set and bottom is golden brown, about 4–6 minutes.
3. Meanwhile, in small bowl combine sour cream, lemon zest, thyme, and pepper and mix well. Sprinkle omelet with Cheddar, cover pan, and remove from heat. Let stand for 3 minutes, then cut into pieces and serve with the sour-cream mixture.

Nutrition Info:
- Info Per Serving: Calories: 243.49; Fat:15.62 g ;Saturated fat: 6.42 g ;Sodium: 354.41 mg

DESSERTS AND TREATS

Peanut Butter And Chia Pudding

Servings: X
Cooking Time: X

Ingredients:

- 2 cups soy milk
- 2 tablespoons natural peanut butter
- 2 tablespoons brown sugar
- 1 teaspoon pure vanilla extract
- Pinch sea salt
- ½ cup chia seeds

Directions:

1. In a medium bowl, whisk together the milk, peanut butter, brown sugar, vanilla, and salt until very smooth and well blended.
2. Stir in the chia seeds, cover the bowl, and refrigerate until the pudding is thick, stirring occasionally, for at least 4 hours.
3. Stir well and serve.

Nutrition Info:

- Info Per Serving: Calories: 500 ; Fat: 31 g ;Saturated fat: 3 g ;Sodium: 292 mg

Choc Chip Banana Muffins

Servings: 8
Cooking Time: 20 Min

Ingredients:

- 2 tbsp. ground flaxseeds
- 5 tbsp. water
- 2 cups almond flour
- 1 tbsp. ground cinnamon
- 1 tsp baking powder
- 3 (1 cup) medium ripe bananas, mashed
- 2 tbsp. organic honey
- ¼ cup dark chocolate chips
- 1 tsp vanilla extract
- ¼ cup unsalted walnuts, chopped

Directions:

1. Heat the oven to 375°F gas mark 5. Line a muffin tin with 8 muffin cup liners. Set aside.
2. In a small-sized mixing bowl, stir in the flaxseeds and water and let this sit for 5 minutes until the mixture congeals.
3. In a large-sized mixing bowl, add the almond flour, cinnamon, and baking powder and mix to combine.
4. In a medium-sized mixing bowl, add the flaxseed mixture, bananas, honey, chocolate chips, and vanilla extract, mix to combine. Slowly pour the wet ingredients into the dry ingredients, mix well. Add in the walnuts and mix.
5. Spoon the mixture evenly into the 8 lined muffin tin, bake for 20 minutes, or until the inserted toothpick comes out clean.
6. Serve warm or once completely cooled, store in an airtight container to stay fresh.

Nutrition Info:

- Info Per Serving: Calories: 199 ; Fat: 5 g ;Saturated fat: 1 g ;Sodium: 64 mg

Chocolate, Peanut Butter, And Banana Ice Cream

Servings: 2
Cooking Time: X

Ingredients:

- 2 frozen bananas, peeled and sliced
- 2 tablespoons cocoa powder
- 1 tablespoon honey
- 2 tablespoons all-natural peanut butter
- 1 tablespoon chopped walnuts (or nut of choice)

Directions:

1. Put the frozen bananas, cocoa powder, honey, and peanut butter into a high-speed blender and blend until smooth.
2. Transfer the ice cream mixture into a resealable container and freeze for 2 hours.
3. Once frozen, scoop the ice cream into two serving bowls and top with walnuts.

Nutrition Info:

- Info Per Serving: Calories: 269 ; Fat: 12 g ;Saturated fat: 2 g ;Sodium: 5 mg

Sweetato Bundt Cake

Servings: 12
Cooking Time: 45 Min

Ingredients:

- Cooking spray
- ¾ cup sweet potato, cooked and mashed
- ½ cup almond milk
- ½ cup brown sugar
- ⅓ cup sunflower oil
- 2 large free-range eggs
- 1¾ cups whole-wheat flour
- ¾ cup quick oats
- 1½ tsp baking powder
- ¾ tsp baking soda
- ¼ tsp ground cinnamon
- ¼ tsp ground nutmeg
- ¼ tsp ground allspice
- ½ cup dark chocolate chips

Directions:

1. Preheat the oven to 350°F gas mark 4.
2. Coat a Bundt cake pan with cooking spray and set aside.
3. In a stand mixer, add the mashed sweet potato, almond milk, sugar, sunflower oil, and eggs, beat until well blended.
4. In a large-sized mixing bowl, add the flour, oats, baking powder, baking soda cinnamon, nutmeg, allspice, and dark chocolate chips, mix to combine.
5. With the stand mixer on low, add 1 soup spoonful at a time of the dry ingredients into the wet ingredients, beat until well combined.
6. Spoon the batter into the prepared Bundt cake pan. Bake for 45 minutes, or until the toothpick inserted comes out clean.
7. Serve or store in an airtight container to stay fresh.

Nutrition Info:

- Info Per Serving: Calories: 242 ; Fat: 10g ;Saturated fat: 3 g ;Sodium: 104 mg

Apple-cinnamon Flatbread

Servings: 5
Cooking Time: 25 Minutes

Ingredients:

- Olive oil, for greasing the pan
- 1½ cups whole wheat or whole-grain self-rising flour
- 1 cup low-fat plain Greek yogurt
- 2 Envy apples, peeled, cored, and thinly sliced
- 2 teaspoons cinnamon
- 1½ tablespoons maple syrup

Directions:

1. Preheat the oven to 350°F. Line a baking sheet with parchment paper and lightly grease it with olive oil.
2. In a medium bowl, mix the flour and yogurt together until smooth, then knead the dough into a ball.
3. Lightly flour your work surface, transfer the dough to the floured surface, and press it into a flat 8-inch circle. Transfer the flattened dough to the prepared baking sheet.
4. In a small bowl, mix the apples and cinnamon until well combined.
5. Arrange the apple slices on the dough and bake until the flatbread is slightly brown on the edges, about 25 minutes.
6. Remove the flatbread from the oven and drizzle with the maple syrup. Enjoy immediately.

Nutrition Info:

- Info Per Serving: Calories: 213; Fat: 2 g ;Saturated fat: 1 g ;Sodium: 37 mg

Balsamic Strawberry Yogurt

Servings: 4
Cooking Time: X

Ingredients:

- 2 cups low-fat unsweetened plain yoghurt
- 1 tbsp. organic honey
- 2 cups strawberries
- 2 tbsp. balsamic vinegar
- 2 tbsp. unsalted walnuts, chopped

Directions:

1. In a small-sized mixing bowl, add the plain yoghurt and organic honey, mix to combine.
2. In another small-sized mixing bowl, add the strawberries and the balsamic vinegar. Use a fork to lightly mash the strawberries in the vinegar. Rest for a few minutes.
3. Serve the yoghurt topped with ½ cup balsamic strawberries and ½ tbsp. walnuts.

Nutrition Info:

- Info Per Serving: Calories: 127 ; Fat: 2 g ;Saturated fat: 1 g ;Sodium: 89 mg

Lemon Floating Island

Servings: 4
Cooking Time: X

Ingredients:

- 2 cups milk
- 6 egg whites
- 2 tablespoons lemon juice
- ½ cup sugar Pinch salt
- 6 tablespoons crushed hard lemon candies, divided
- 1 recipe Lemon Mousse

Directions:

1. Preheat oven to 275ºF. In large skillet, place milk and bring to a simmer over medium heat. Reduce heat to low.

2. Meanwhile, in large bowl combine egg whites and lemon juice; beat until foamy. Gradually add sugar and salt, beating until very stiff peaks form. Fold in 3 tablespoons of the crushed candies.

3. With a large spoon, scoop out about ¼ cup of the egg white mixture and gently place in the simmering milk. Poach for 2 minutes, then carefully turn each meringue and poach for another 2 minutes. Remove from heat, drain briefly on kitchen towel, and place on Silpat-lined cookie sheets. Repeat with remaining egg white mixture.

4. Bake meringues for 12–16 minutes or until they puff slightly and start to turn light golden brown. Remove and refrigerate, uncovered, for 1–2 hours before serving.

5. When you prepare the Lemon Mousse, spoon the mousse into individual custard cups; chill until firm. Top each with a poached meringue, sprinkle with remaining 3 tablespoons crushed candies, and serve immediately.

Nutrition Info:

- Info Per Serving: Calories: 295.74; Fat:0.80 g ;Saturated fat: 0.45 g;Sodium:190.06 mg

Chocolate-butterscotch Parfaits

Servings: 6
Cooking Time: X

Ingredients:

- 1 recipe Silken Chocolate Mousse
- 10 Butterscotch Meringues
- 6 tablespoons chopped hazelnuts, toasted
- 6 tablespoons butterscotch ice cream topping

Directions:

1. Prepare Silken Chocolate Mousse and refrigerate for 2 hours, until set. Prepare Butterscotch Meringues and let cool completely.

2. Break up meringues with your fingers. In six large parfait glasses, layer mousse and meringue crumbs, ending with the mousse. Sprinkle with toasted hazelnuts, cover, and chill for 2–4 hours.

3. Drizzle each parfait with 1 tablespoon butterscotch ice cream topping just before serving.

Nutrition Info:

- Info Per Serving: Calories: 365.51; Fat: 16.62 g ;Saturated fat: 8.27 g;Sodium: 179.64 mg

Blueberry-hazelnut Crisp

Servings: 8
Cooking Time: X

Ingredients:

- 3 cups blueberries
- ¼ cup sugar
- 1 teaspoon cinnamon
- ½ teaspoon nutmeg
- 1½ cups quick-cooking oatmeal
- ½ cup flour
- ¼ cup whole-wheat flour
- ½ cup brown sugar
- ½ cup chopped hazelnuts
- 1/3 cup butter or margarine, melted

Directions:

1. Preheat oven to 350ºF. Spray a 9" round cake pan with nonstick cooking spray and set aside.

2. Combine blueberries in medium bowl with sugar, cinnamon, and nutmeg. Spoon into prepared pan.

3. In same bowl, combine oatmeal, flour, whole-wheat flour, brown sugar, and hazelnuts and mix well. Add melted butter and mix until crumbly. Sprinkle over fruit in dish.

4. Bake for 35–45 minutes or until fruit bubbles and topping is browned and crisp. Let cool for 15 minutes before serving.

Nutrition Info:

- Info Per Serving: Calories:373.56; Fat:14.57 g ;Saturated fat: 5.59 g;Sodium: 61.35 mg

Apple-date Turnovers

Servings: 12
Cooking Time: X

Ingredients:
- 2 Granny Smith apples, peeled and chopped
- ½ cup finely chopped dates
- 1 teaspoon lemon juice
- 1 tablespoon flour
- 3 tablespoons brown sugar
- 1½ teaspoons cinnamon, divided
- 8 (14" × 18") sheets frozen filo dough, thawed
- ½ cup finely chopped walnuts
- 5 tablespoons sugar, divided
- 1/3 cup butter or margarine, melted

Directions:
1. In medium bowl, combine apples, dates, lemon juice, flour, brown sugar, and 1 teaspoon cinnamon, and mix well; set aside. Place thawed filo dough on work surface and cover with a damp kitchen towel to prevent drying. Work with one sheet at a time. In small bowl, combine walnuts and 3 tablespoons sugar.
2. Lay one sheet filo on work surface; brush with butter. Sprinkle with 2 tablespoons of the walnut mixture. Place another sheet of filo on top, brush with butter, and sprinkle with 1 tablespoon of the walnut mixture. Cut into three 4¼" × 18" strips.
3. Place 2 tablespoons of the apple filling at one end of dough strips. Fold a corner of the dough over the filling so edges match, then continue folding dough as you would fold a flag. Place on ungreased cookie sheets and brush with more butter. Repeat process with remaining strips.
4. Preheat oven to 375ºF. In small bowl, combine remaining 2 tablespoons sugar and ½ teaspoon cinnamon and mix well. Sprinkle over turnovers. Bake for 20 to 30 minutes or until pastries are golden brown and crisp. Remove to wire racks to cool.

Nutrition Info:
- Info Per Serving: Calories: 182.02; Fat: 9.01 g ;Saturated fat:3.61 g;Sodium:99.11mg

Curried Fruit Compote

Servings: 6
Cooking Time: 10 Minutes

Ingredients:
- 1 (8-ounce) can pineapple chunks, undrained
- 1 ripe pear, peeled and chopped
- 1 Granny Smith apple, chopped
- ⅓ cup dried cranberries
- 1 cup apple juice
- 1 tablespoon fresh lemon juice
- 2 tablespoons agave nectar or packed brown sugar
- 1 tablespoon curry powder
- 1 tablespoon cornstarch
- Pinch salt

Directions:
1. In a medium saucepan over medium heat, combine the pineapple chunks, pear, apple, cranberries, apple juice, lemon juice, agave nectar (or brown sugar), curry powder, cornstarch, and salt. Stir to blend.
2. Bring to a boil, reduce the heat to low, and simmer for 6 to 8 minutes or until the fruit is tender.
3. At this point, you can serve the compote as-is, or you can purée all—or part—of it. The compote can be stored in the refrigerator for up to 3 days. You can re-warm the compote on the stovetop before you serve it.

Nutrition Info:
- Info Per Serving: Calories: 112 ; Fat: 0 g ;Saturated fat: 0 g ;Sodium: 4 mg

Strawberry-rhubarb Parfait

Servings: 6
Cooking Time: X

Ingredients:
- 2 stalks rhubarb, sliced
- ½ cup apple juice
- 1/3 cup sugar
- 1 (10-ounce) package frozen strawberries
- 3 cups frozen vanilla yogurt

Directions:
1. In medium saucepan, combine rhubarb, apple juice, and sugar. Bring to a simmer, then reduce heat and simmer for 8–10 minutes or until rhubarb is soft.
2. Remove pan from heat and immediately stir in frozen strawberries, stirring to break up strawberries. Let stand until cool, about 30 minutes.
3. Layer rhubarb mixture and frozen yogurt in parfait glasses or goblets, starting and ending with rhubarb mixture. Cover and freeze until firm, about 8 hours.

Nutrition Info:
- Info Per Serving: Calories:210.56; Fat: 4.16 g ;Saturated fat: 2.48 g;Sodium: 64.41 mg

Skillet Apple Crisp With Mixed Nuts

Servings: 4
Cooking Time: 15 Minutes

Ingredients:
• 2 large Granny Smith or Gala apples, cored and sliced ½ inch thick
• 4 tablespoons apple juice, divided
• 3 tablespoons granulated sugar
• 2 tablespoons salted butter, divided
• 1 tablespoon cornstarch
• ¼ cup packed brown sugar
• ½ cup rolled oats
• 2 tablespoons almond flour
• ½ teaspoon ground cinnamon
• ⅛ teaspoon ground nutmeg
• 1 tablespoon sliced almonds
• 1 tablespoon chopped pecans

Directions:
1. In a nonstick skillet over medium heat, combine the apples, 1 tablespoon of the apple juice, granulated sugar, and 1 tablespoon of the butter.
2. Bring the apple mixture to a simmer, reduce the heat to low, and cook for 8 to 9 minutes, stirring occasionally, until the fruit is tender.
3. In a small bowl, combine 2 tablespoons of the apple juice and the cornstarch. Stir into the apple mixture and simmer for 1 minute longer or until thickened and tender.
4. Meanwhile, in a medium bowl, combine the brown sugar, oats, almond flour, cinnamon, and nutmeg. To the oat mixture, add the remaining 1 tablespoon butter along with the remaining 3 tablespoons of the apple juice, and mix until crumbly. Stir in the almonds and pecans.
5. Put the oat mixture in another skillet over medium heat and cook until the mixture is toasted and slightly browner, about 4 to 5 minutes. Remove from the heat and transfer onto a plate.
6. When the apples are tender, top with the oat mixture and serve.

Nutrition Info:
• Info Per Serving: Calories: 272 ; Fat: 11 g ;Saturated fat: 5 g ;Sodium: 45 mg

Butterscotch Meringues

Servings: 30
Cooking Time: X

Ingredients:
• 3 egg whites Pinch of salt
• ¼ teaspoon cream of tartar
• 2/3 cup sugar
• 2 tablespoons brown sugar
• 10 round hard butterscotch candies, finely crushed

Directions:
1. Preheat oven to 250ºF. In large bowl, beat egg whites with salt and cream of tartar until foamy. Gradually beat in sugar and brown sugar until stiff peaks form and sugar is dissolved. Fold in the finely crushed candies.
2. Drop by teaspoonfuls onto a baking sheet lined with aluminum foil or Silpat liners. Bake for 50–60 minutes or until meringues are set and crisp and very light golden brown. Cool on the cookie sheets for 3 minutes, then carefully peel off the foil and place on wire racks to cool.

Nutrition Info:
• Info Per Serving: Calories:29.39; Fat:0.06 g ;Saturated fat:0.04 g;Sodium: 17.97 mg

Blueberry Crumble

Servings: 5
Cooking Time: 20 Minutes

Ingredients:
• 3 tablespoons olive oil, plus extra for greasing the baking pan
• ½ cup chopped walnuts
• 1 cup pitted Medjool dates
• 1 cup steel-cut oats
• 1½ cups blueberries
• 1½ tablespoons honey

Directions:
1. Preheat the oven to 350°F. Lightly oil an 8-inch-square baking pan.
2. In a food processor or blender, pulse the walnuts until they are finely ground. Transfer to a medium bowl and set aside.
3. Place the dates in the food processor and pulse until they become a coarse paste. Transfer to the bowl and mix with the walnuts.
4. Add the oats and the olive oil to the bowl and mix until the mixture sticks together.
5. Press half of the oat mixture into the bottom of the prepared baking pan.
6. Spread the blueberries evenly over the oat mixture and drizzle with the honey. Top with the remaining

half of the oat mixture.

7. Bake for 20 minutes until the berries are bubbly. Enjoy immediately.

Nutrition Info:

• Info Per Serving: Calories:375 ; Fat: 17 g ;Saturated fat: 2g ;Sodium: 2 mg

Pumpkin Pie Fruit Leathers

Servings: 10
Cooking Time: 8 Hours

Ingredients:

• 2 cups pumpkin purée
• 1 cup unsweetened applesauce
• 1 tablespoon maple syrup
• ¼ teaspoon ground cinnamon
• ⅛ teaspoon ground nutmeg
• ⅛ teaspoon ground ginger
• Pinch ground allspice

Directions:

1. Preheat the oven to the lowest setting possible or 150oF.
2. Line a baking sheet with parchment paper and set aside.
3. In a medium bowl, whisk together the pumpkin, applesauce, maple syrup, cinnamon, nutmeg, ginger, and allspice until very well blended. Spread the mixture on the baking sheet as evenly and thinly as possible.
4. Place the baking sheet in the oven and bake until the mixture is completely dried and no longer tacky to the touch, about 8 hours.
5. Remove the leather from the oven and cut into 10 pieces.

Nutrition Info:

• Info Per Serving: Calories: 33 ; Fat: 0 g ;Saturated fat: 0 g ;Sodium: 3 mg

Fruit Yoghurt Parfait

Servings: 2
Cooking Time: 20 Min

Ingredients:

• 2 cups plain Greek yogurt
• 1 banana, sliced
• ½ cup strawberries, sliced
• ¼ cup almonds, chopped
• ¼ cup unsalted sunflower seeds, roasted
• 2 tbsp. organic honey

• 1 tbsp. chia seeds, for garnish
• 1 tbsp. small dark chocolate chips, for garnish

Directions:

1. Divide the yoghurt between two serving bowls.
2. Evenly divide the banana, strawberries, almonds, and roasted sunflower seeds between the bowls.
3. Drizzle each bowl with 1 tbsp. of honey and top them with chia seeds and chocolate chips.
4. Serve cold.

Nutrition Info:

• Info Per Serving: Calories: 394 ; Fat: 18 g ;Saturated fat: 2 g ;Sodium: 57 mg

Loco Pie Crust

Servings: 8
Cooking Time: X

Ingredients:

• ½ cup plus
• 1 tablespoon mayonnaise
• 3 tablespoons buttermilk
• 1 teaspoon vinegar
• 1½ cups flour

Directions:

1. In large bowl, combine mayonnaise, buttermilk, and vinegar and mix well. Add flour, stirring with a fork to form a ball. You may need to add more buttermilk or more flour to make a workable dough. Press dough into a ball, wrap in plastic wrap, and refrigerate for 1 hour.
2. When ready to bake, preheat oven to 400ºF. Roll out dough between two sheets of waxed paper. Remove top sheet and place crust in 9" pie pan. Carefully ease off the top sheet of paper, then ease the crust into the pan and press to bottom and sides. Fold edges under and flute.
3. Either use as recipe directs, or bake for 5 minutes, then press crust down with fork if necessary. Bake for 5–8 minutes longer or until crust is light golden brown.

Nutrition Info:

• Info Per Serving: Calories:171.83; Fat: 7.35 g ;Saturated fat:1.18 g;Sodium: 65.46 mg

Chocolate Banana Caramel Pudding

Servings: 4
Cooking Time: 15 Minutes

Ingredients:

- 2 ripe bananas, cut into 1-inch chunks (see Ingredient Tip)
- ¼ cup cocoa powder, plus more to adjust chocolate level
- ¼ cup low-fat soy milk
- 2 tablespoons vanilla protein powder
- 2 tablespoons caramel sauce
- ½ teaspoon vanilla extract
- Pinch salt
- 2 tablespoons mini semisweet chocolate chips

Directions:

1. In a blender or food processor, combine the bananas, cocoa powder, soy milk, protein powder, caramel sauce, vanilla, and salt, and blend or process until smooth.
2. Add more cocoa, about a tablespoon at a time, if you'd like a darker chocolate pudding or to adjust the chocolate flavor.
3. Pour into 4 small cups and top each with the chocolate chips, then serve. Or you can cover the puddings and chill for 2 to 3 hours before serving.

Nutrition Info:

- Info Per Serving: Calories: 164 ; Fat: 4 g ;Saturated fat: 2 g ;Sodium: 29 mg

Whole-wheat Chocolate Chip Cookies

Servings: 48
Cooking Time: X

Ingredients:

- ¼ cup butter or plant sterol margarine, softened
- 1½ cups brown sugar
- ½ cup applesauce
- 1 tablespoon vanilla
- 1 egg
- 2 egg whites
- 2½ cups whole-wheat pastry flour
- ½ cup ground oatmeal
- 1 teaspoon baking soda
- ¼ teaspoon salt
- 2 cups special dark chocolate chips
- 1 cup chopped hazelnuts

Directions:

1. Preheat oven to 375ºF. Line cookie sheets with parchment paper or Sil-pat silicone liners and set aside.
2. In large bowl, combine butter, brown sugar, and applesauce and beat well until smooth. Add vanilla, egg, and egg whites and beat until combined.
3. Add flour, oatmeal, baking soda, and salt and mix until a dough forms. Fold in chocolate chips and hazelnuts.
4. Drop dough by rounded teaspoons onto prepared cookie sheets. Bake for 7–10 minutes or until cookies are light golden brown and set. Let cool for 5 minutes before removing from cookie sheet to wire rack to cool.

Nutrition Info:

- Info Per Serving: Calories: 114.86; Fat:4.89 g ;Saturated fat:2.04 g;Sodium:26.49 mg

Apple Pear-nut Crisp

Servings: 8
Cooking Time: X

Ingredients:

- 2 apples, sliced
- 3 pears, sliced
- 2 tablespoons lemon juice
- ¼ cup sugar
- 1 teaspoon cinnamon
- ½ teaspoon nutmeg
- 1½ cups quick-cooking oatmeal
- ½ cup flour
- ¼ cup whole-wheat flour
- ½ cup brown sugar
- 1/3 cup butter or margarine, melted

Directions:

1. Preheat oven to 350ºF. Spray a 9" round cake pan with nonstick cooking spray and set aside.
2. Prepare apples and pears, sprinkling with lemon juice as you work. Combine in medium bowl with sugar, cinnamon, and nutmeg. Spoon into prepared cake pan.
3. In same bowl, combine oatmeal, flour, whole-wheat flour, and brown sugar and mix well. Add melted butter and mix until crumbly. Sprinkle over fruit in dish.
4. Bake for 35–45 minutes or until fruit bubbles and topping is browned and crisp. Let cool for 15 minutes before serving.

Nutrition Info:

- Info Per Serving: Calories: 353.77; Fat:9.97 g ;Saturated fat: 5.25 g;Sodium: 61.78 mg

Double Chocolate Cinnamon Nice Cream

Servings: 4
Cooking Time: 5 Minutes

Ingredients:

- 3 tablespoons semisweet chocolate chips
- 2 frozen bananas, cut into chunks
- ⅓ cup frozen mango cubes
- 2 Medjool dates, pit removed and chopped (see Ingredient Tip)
- 2 tablespoons flax or soy milk
- 3 tablespoons cocoa powder
- ½ teaspoon vanilla extract
- ½ teaspoon ground cinnamon
- Pinch salt

Directions:

1. In a small saucepan over low heat, melt the semisweet chocolate chips, stirring frequently. Transfer the melted chocolate from the pan to a small bowl to cool, and place it in the refrigerator while you prepare the rest of the ingredients. (Make sure to not let the chocolate harden.)
2. In a blender or food processor, combine the bananas, mangoes, dates, and milk and blend until well combined.
3. Add the cocoa powder, vanilla, cinnamon, salt, and the melted, cooled chocolate. Blend until the mixture is smooth.
4. This treat can be served right away or frozen for 2 to 3 hours before serving.

Nutrition Info:

- Info Per Serving: Calories: 221 ; Fat: 5 g ;Saturated fat: 4 g ;Sodium: 8 mg

Almond Cheesecake–stuffed Apples

Servings: X
Cooking Time: 25 Minutes

Ingredients:

- 2 small apples, cut in half and cores scooped out on each side
- 1 teaspoon canola oil
- 2 tablespoons brown sugar, divided
- ⅛ teaspoon ground cinnamon
- ¼ cup fat-free cream cheese
- ⅛ teaspoon almond extract
- 2 tablespoons chopped almonds, for garnish

Directions:

1. Preheat the oven to 400°F.
2. Line a small baking dish with parchment paper and arrange the apple halves in the dish, cut-side up.
3. Brush the cut side of the apples with the canola oil. Sprinkle 1 tablespoon brown sugar and the cinnamon over the halves.
4. Place in the oven and bake for 15 minutes.
5. While the apples are baking, in a small bowl, stir together the cream cheese, remaining 1 tablespoon brown sugar, and almond extract until well blended.
6. Evenly divide the cream cheese mixture among the apple halves and bake for 10 more minutes.
7. Top with almonds and serve.

Nutrition Info:

- Info Per Serving: Calories: 307 ; Fat: 16 g ;Saturated fat: 7 g ;Sodium: 90 mg

Appendix A : Measurement Conversions

BASIC KITCHEN CONVERSIONS & EQUIVALENTS

DRY MEASUREMENTS CONVERSION CHART

3 TEASPOONS = 1 TABLESPOON = 1/16 CUP

6 TEASPOONS = 2 TABLESPOONS = 1/8 CUP

12 TEASPOONS = 4 TABLESPOONS = 1/4 CUP

24 TEASPOONS = 8 TABLESPOONS = 1/2 CUP

36 TEASPOONS = 12 TABLESPOONS = 3/4 CUP

48 TEASPOONS = 16 TABLESPOONS = 1 CUP

METRIC TO US COOKING CONVERSIONS

OVEN TEMPERATURES

120 °C = 250 °F

160 °C = 320 °F

180° C = 350 °F

205 °C = 400 °F

220 °C = 425 °F

LIQUID MEASUREMENTS CONVERSION CHART

8 FLUID OUNCES = 1 CUP = 1/2 PINT = 1/4 QUART

16 FLUID OUNCES = 2 CUPS = 1 PINT = 1/2 QUART

32 FLUID OUNCES = 4 CUPS = 2 PINTS = 1 QUART = 1/4 GALLON

128 FLUID OUNCES = 16 CUPS = 8 PINTS = 4 QUARTS = 1 GALLON

BAKING IN GRAMS

1 CUP FLOUR = 140 GRAMS

1 CUP SUGAR = 150 GRAMS

1 CUP POWDERED SUGAR = 160 GRAMS

1 CUP HEAVY CREAM = 235 GRAMS

VOLUME

1 MILLILITER = 1/5 TEASPOON

5 ML = 1 TEASPOON

15 ML = 1 TABLESPOON

240 ML = 1 CUP OR 8 FLUID OUNCES

1 LITER = 34 FL. OUNCES

WEIGHT

1 GRAM = .035 OUNCES

100 GRAMS = 3.5 OUNCES

500 GRAMS = 1.1 POUNDS

1 KILOGRAM = 35 OUNCES

US TO METRIC COOKING CONVERSIONS

1/5 TSP = 1 ML

1 TSP = 5 ML

1 TBSP = 15 ML

1 FL OUNCE = 30 ML

1 CUP = 237 ML

1 PINT (2 CUPS) = 473 ML

1 QUART (4 CUPS) = .95 LITER

1 GALLON (16 CUPS) = 3.8 LITERS

1 OZ = 28 GRAMS

1 POUND = 454 GRAMS

BUTTER

1 CUP BUTTER = 2 STICKS = 8 OUNCES = 230 GRAMS = 8 TABLESPOONS

WHAT DOES 1 CUP EQUAL

1 CUP = 8 FLUID OUNCES

1 CUP = 16 TABLESPOONS

1 CUP = 48 TEASPOONS

1 CUP = 1/2 PINT

1 CUP = 1/4 QUART

1 CUP = 1/16 GALLON

1 CUP = 240 ML

BAKING PAN CONVERSIONS

1 CUP ALL-PURPOSE FLOUR = 4.5 OZ

1 CUP ROLLED OATS = 3 OZ 1 LARGE EGG = 1.7 OZ

1 CUP BUTTER = 8 OZ 1 CUP MILK = 8 OZ

1 CUP HEAVY CREAM = 8.4 OZ

1 CUP GRANULATED SUGAR = 7.1 OZ

1 CUP PACKED BROWN SUGAR = 7.75 OZ

1 CUP VEGETABLE OIL = 7.7 OZ

1 CUP UNSIFTED POWDERED SUGAR = 4.4 OZ

BAKING PAN CONVERSIONS

9-INCH ROUND CAKE PAN = 12 CUPS

10-INCH TUBE PAN =16 CUPS

11-INCH BUNDT PAN = 12 CUPS

9-INCH SPRINGFORM PAN = 10 CUPS

9 X 5 INCH LOAF PAN = 8 CUPS

9-INCH SQUARE PAN = 8 CUPS

Appendix B : Recipes Index

D

E

F

G

H

I

K

L

R

S

T

V

W

Z

Made in the USA
Las Vegas, NV
16 October 2023